D0561294

AM I THE LEADER
I NEED TO BE?

by Harold C. Lloyd

Raphel Marketing
118 S. Newton Place
Atlantic City, NJ 08401

Am I The Leader I Need to Be?

Copyright © 2008 by Harold C. Lloyd

Published by: Raphel Marketing,
118 S. Newton Place, Atlantic City, NJ 08401

Cover Design and Illustrations by: Chris Murphy
Book Design by: The Graphic Design Factory

Manufactured in the United States of America
ISBN 0-9711542-5-2

Other Raphel Marketing Books Include:
Win the Customer, NOT the Argument by Don Gallegos
Speaking Rules! by Murray Raphel
Selling Rules! by Murray Raphel
Crowning the Customer by Feargal Quinn
Loyalty Marketing: The Second Act by Brian Woolf

For more information on these books and for quantity purchases of
Am I The Leader I Need to Be?
please contact:
Raphel Marketing
118 S. Newton Place, Atlantic City, NJ 08401
Toll-Free: 877-386-5925
Phone: 609-348-6646   Fax: 609-347-2455
Email: neil@raphel.com   Website: www.raphel.com

CONTENTS

Page

Introduction

THANK YOU! THANK YOU! THANK YOU!

I would like to first acknowledge the scores of people who have professed appreciation for the material contained in my seminar, "Am I The Leader I Need To Be?" and asked for more. Their enthusiasm and support ignited my desire to transform a 90-minute seminar into a book that encapsulates a significant portion of my life's work.

The next credit goes to Gail Steven, my assistant for over 20 years (and my mother-in-law), who literally transformed my scribbles into pages of words that, when pasted together, began to look like a book.

Acknowledgement number three has to go to Toni Boyle, an accomplished author herself. Toni took Gail's pages and magically transformed them into grammatically correct sentences with clear meaning. She is an extremely gifted individual who made me relive the time I spent in eighth grade English.

The fourth step in the process of making this book was carried out by my team of "proofreaders": Tom Schulte, Erika Swanson, David Zallie, Carol Christison, Sam Corea, Sue Cohen, P. K. Hoover, Deanna Lloyd, and Ernie Monschein. Their critical and constructive comments were invaluable.

Chris Murphy was a major contributor to this project. He was given the responsibility of creating some fun visual breaks among all the pages of words. Chris is a talented cartoonist, and he did a superb job.

The next acknowledgement is for all the employees, students, and associates I've had the distinct pleasure of interacting with over the years. You've given me the life experiences I treasure – the experiences that have enabled me to create this book.

The most special acknowledgement goes to my "Fab Four." To Deanna, my wife, whose love, support, and understanding is always unwavering. To Deanna, our first-born, who showed me that being a parent is everything I dreamed it would be. To Randee, who convinced me that having two children is three times more fun. To Alex, who made us an odd number (5), but an even better family. This Fabulous Four has blessed me with the best times of my life.

The final acknowledgement goes to Murray and Neil Raphel, whose company, Raphel Marketing, is charged with the responsibility of getting as many people to read *Am I The Leader I Need To Be?* as possible. Their efforts will ensure that the Make-A-Wish Foundation gains the most from the financial success of this book.

In summary, a Manager works hard to get others to see the light, while a Leader generates the light by harnessing the energies of others.

It should also be mentioned that a leader sometimes manages and a manager occasionally leads. The principles of leadership I teach can be used by a leader, a manager, or even a participant who may at times be put in a position to lead.

4. This Leadership Book Distinguishes Genuine Leaders from Pretenders

The principles of leadership aren't confined to business organizations or the military. A leader is truly anyone with the responsibility to propel others toward a common objective. Some people do this better than others. I've found that there are many people who have the title and do the job adequately but don't have the passion and skill of a Genuine Leader. These "wannabe" commanders are what I call "Pretenders." They're playing a role without understanding how to be really effective, and they often do more harm than good.

Throughout this book, you'll see how Genuine Leaders differ from their Pretender counterparts and that Pretenders can morph into Genuine Leaders if they embrace the advice and principles in the proceeding chapters. This book is fundamental and practical, chock-full of ideas that can be used in any number of leadership scenarios.

Aren't 220,137 Enough?

When I first met with my editor to discuss working together on this book, she pointed out that Amazon.com already cited 220,137 titles on the subject and asked, "Does the world really need another book on leadership?" My immediate reaction was an emphatic "YES!" because I have read a lot of those other titles and found very little that applied to the leadership roles that most of us fill every day. In fact, there are six major differences that I see between this book and all those other titles on the shelf.

1. This Book on Leadership Isn't for CEOs of Big Corporations

Most leadership books seem to be written either by leaders of huge corporations or by business professors who relate case studies based on those companies. Those books are not written for the unsung heroes who manage day-to-day operations in businesses large and small. I'm writing for the leaders and future leaders who spend most of their time on the firing line – the men and women whose subordinates look to them for direction, clarity and inspiration.

There's a vast difference between leading a workforce of MBAs from the nation's top universities and generating enthusiasm in a group of high school graduates who are trying to earn enough to attend college one day. I especially want to help those of you who are leading organizations with hourly workers or volunteers, whether they're young, part-time, or seasonal. You have your work cut out for you, and this work is just as important as anything faced by Lee Iacocca at Chrysler or Jack Welch at General Electric. The major difference between the leaders of mega-corporations and you is that you have less help, more immediate decisions to make, and a smaller budget.

2. This Leadership Book is by a Leader Who Has Led

It's great to have an education in business (I have a BS in Economics from the University of Pennsylvania, Wharton School and a MBA from the University of Chicago), but all the book learning in the world doesn't add up to a hill of beans if you haven't spent time working the same jobs your team is asked to perform. I've interacted with, consulted for, and learned from several accomplished leaders over the past 20 years, but it's equally important that I have also:

1. Led a company of 80 managers and 1,000 employees.
2. Spent seven years teaching college students.
3. Led 2000+ management seminars.
4. Run a three-unit restaurant franchise with 170 employees.
5. Quarterbacked a football team.
6. Pitched for a championship softball team.
7. Been a husband and father to a fabulous family of five.

If you're going to write about or teach a subject, it's better to have done it than to have only read about it or researched it. I've made some good and some bad decisions, but in the end, I've learned valuable lessons from both – and hopefully, so will you.

3. This Leadership Book Distinguishes Between a Manager and a Leader

In any organization, there are four types of people: leaders, managers, participants, and detractors. Although I'm writing primarily for leaders and future leaders, it's important to clearly differentiate between the roles of a leader and a manager. Too often we use these titles interchangeably – or worse, as antonyms, when a leader is deemed superior to a manager.

You've probably heard the common two-sentence comparison between a leader and a manager:

> A good *manager* does things right.
> A good *leader* does the right things.

It's true that leaders and managers play important, albeit different, roles. So what is the difference?

A Manager	A Leader
1. Plans for today, tomorrow, and the rest of the week. Occasionally conducts meetings that are primarily informational.	1. Plans for next month and next year. Utilizes meetings to solve problems, make decisions, and achieve group understanding.
2. Organizes people around tasks by using To-Do lists.	2. Organizes people around a mission and a set of goals.
3. Gives direction with directives, adhering to a checklist.	3. Prefers that associates become self-directed with a shared vision.
4. Controls the staff by creating a structured work environment utilizing basic recognition and discipline techniques.	4. Controls the organization by creating a motivating working environment of collaboration and choi

A Genuine Leader is...	**A Pretender is...**
➥ A positive influence with a physical presence that is ubiquitous	✗ A stealth bomber, seen only when some negative feedback needs to be dumped
➥ One who thinks of ways to make people more focused on company goals	✗ One who thinks of personal status and is self-serving
➥ Comfortable with people in the workplace	✗ Uncomfortable with people
➥ Open and available to all	✗ Inaccessible, especially to subordinates
➥ Fair to all	✗ Fair only to those who will return a favor
➥ Decisive	✗ A procrastinator
➥ Tough and willing to confront nasty problems	✗ Elusive and an avoider
➥ Persistent	✗ Persistent only when personal gain is to be had
➥ One who simplifies things	✗ One who complicates things
➥ Tolerant of open disagreements	✗ Intolerant of dissent
➥ A sharer of resources and information	✗ One who holds all the cards and shares nothing
➥ One who pitches in when necessary	✗ "Above" pitching in
➥ Trusting	✗ Distrustful
➥ Free to give credit	✗ One who takes the credit
➥ Honest with all associates	✗ Manipulative
➥ A developer of talent within	✗ One who complains about the lack of good people
➥ Steadfast; decisive under pressure	✗ Purposely ambiguous
➥ A face-to-face communicator	✗ Exclusively a memo writer and e-mailer
➥ Consistent and credible	✗ Unpredictable, erratic and deceptive
➥ One who admits own mistakes and comforts others when they make and admit theirs	✗ One who "never" makes mistakes and criticizes others for theirs

5. This Leadership Book Is a "Leader Meter."

During our school years, most of us were exposed to three common grading systems: 1–100 scoring, A-to-F measurement, and the Pass/Fail approach. I remember how I felt if I received a 79 on a test. I couldn't wait to scrutinize it for a grading error so I could get an extra point or two to bring the grade up over an 80. When I received a C+, I was less inclined to fight for a higher grade. And when I received a "P" under the Pass/Fail system, I never even considered reviewing the paper. I'd think, "Why bother? I passed, didn't I?"

As a teacher, I found that people almost always become more involved in the learning process when number grades are used, which is why I feel it's vital to quantify your ability to lead, using a numerical score. The more specific we are with our grade (i.e., 1–100 vs. Pass/Fail), the more inclined we are to work on improving it. It is, without a doubt, easier to manage something that is easily and specifically measured.

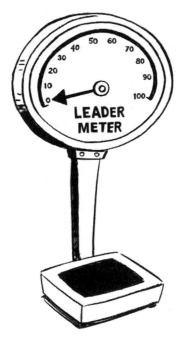

Here's a simple example that explains my theory. If you decide to go on a diet, you will probably consider the following two questions:

How much do I weigh now?
How much do I want to lose?

"Too much" (question 1) and "A lot" (question 2) are typical responses.

Notice that without a specific answer to the first question, it's almost impossible to measure your progress toward a goal. Without a benchmark, you have no baseline for comparison, and your diet is therefore likely to fail. If you say, "I weigh 200 pounds now and I want to lose 20 pounds," you have a measurable and manageable goal.

In this book, we'll be looking at the eleven characteristics of a Genuine Leader. At the end of each chapter, you'll be asked to rate yourself on that characteristic. Then, at the end of the book, you will total all eleven scores to determine your "Leadership Quotient" (LQ), which is similar to an IQ score, but measures your ability to lead.

But before we begin Chapter 1, take a moment to think of your leadership ability today. What would you estimate your leadership score is at this moment? Using our scale from 1 to 100, write your estimated leadership score in the box below.

My Estimated Benchmark Leadership Score today is:

Today's Date:_____

This benchmark score should be as honest as your ego, insight, and humility will permit. The more accurate you are in your estimate, the more interesting this book will be for you.

I've discovered scores will tend to be lower if you...
- Are new to the work force
- Are new to your job
- Are more modest or insecure
- Have been recently involved in an organizational down-sizing
- Have been exposed to some really great leaders and feel humbled

On the other hand, scores will tend to be higher if you...
- Have established a long and credible reputation in your particular field
- Have been favorably reviewed by your superiors in the past
- Are a wishful thinker
- Are a little too confident
- Have met very few Genuine Leaders to use as a comparison

It's very likely that you're already earning a passing grade as a leader. Consequently, you're probably not working as hard as you could be to get better. But imagine how much harder you would work to improve if you knew your Leadership Quotient (LQ) was a specific number and that it was a few points shy of your desired score. That's why a Pass/Fail attitude is not nearly as effective as our Leader Meter's 1–100 scale.

6. This Leadership Book Has Been Test-Driven.

Many of the ideas in this book are from my 90-minute seminar of the same title that I've been teaching for 4 years. By all reports, the seminar version has positively impacted many people's lives. I've heard feedback like, "I'm recommitting...", "I'm reevaluating...", and " I'm rethinking..." from many participants.

So, in a sense, the material in this book has already been test-driven. As long as you're willing to put your mind and your heart into it, these ideas can take you wherever you want to go as a Genuine Leader. Reading this book will be an interesting expedition of self-improvement. Enjoy the journey!

CHAPTER 1

GENUINE LEADERS HAVE VISION AND PASSION

The most pathetic person in the world
is someone who has sight, but no vision.

Helen Keller, American author, activist, and lecturer

When I acquired the development rights for a family-style restaurant in Virginia Beach, Virginia, my first act was to send a deposit check of $5,000 to the franchisor. My second act was to plan a trip to Stuart, Florida. I wanted to see one of the Blake brothers who had founded the chain some 63 years earlier.

When I learned that Pres Blake was amenable to my visit, I jumped at the opportunity. For me, part of the allure of the franchise was its heritage. I made the trip to Stuart, two hours south of Orlando, with my director of operations. As we sat in the living room with Pres, his passion for the business, even though he had retired long ago, lit up the room.

He talked about the importance of taking care of the customers, treating employees as valuable assets, and offering high quality products. I was especially moved when he told us how his close friend, J. C. Penney, had convinced Pres that it is possible to be a man of integrity and still succeed in business.

Because of our pilgrimage to visit the Blakes, we were able to absorb the founder's vision and could better convey to our employees our motivation for continuing the franchise. And it was certainly an honor for all of us when Pres and his wife Helen visited Virginia Beach to cut the ribbon at our grand opening.

The Six Vital Questions

If an organization is to be successful, it must have a set of shared values, a clear vision, and a defined mission. In forming any type of purposeful organization, Genuine Leaders must answer these **Six Vital Questions**:

Who am I?
Who are we?
What do we stand for?
Where are we going?
How are we going to get there?
What needs to get done, and when do we begin?

Question 1. Who am I?

Your work ethic, your passion, your personal integrity and honesty toward others define a large part of your character. You must understand your own motivation in business – why you do what you do – before you can hope to lead other people. Make sure your personal goals mesh with the goals you set for your company. In Chapter Five, we will discuss the subject of honesty and integrity in depth.

Question 2. Who are we?

We can answer this question by using a **values statement**. Shared values define a group. Values can include such qualities as unquestionable honesty, dedication to the community, offering only top-notch goods, being respectful of others, and maintaining a "fun" environment in the workplace. In my foodservice business, our associates' shared values were:

1. Be Honest, Always. *(To Us, Your Guests and Yourself)*
2. Tell Us What's Bothering You. *(We Care and Want to Help)*
3. Encourage Others. *(Compliment 10 People Every Day)*
4. Never Criticize a Suggestion. *(Without Offering an Option)*
5. Keep Your Promises. *(Even the Smallest Ones)*
6. Think Safety. *(Please Wipe Up That Spill)*
7. Think Clean. *(Please Clean Under That Table)*
8. Please Don't "Cuss." *(Or Otherwise Offend)*
9. Say "Please" and "Thank You." *(Often)*
10. Smile a Lot. *(Make a Positive Impact)*

Question 3. What do we stand for?

What is our vision? Why does our organization exist? What is its purpose?

Leaders use **vision statements** to elucidate their purposes. A good vision statement encapsulates the reason for the organization's existence. It can be as short as a few words or as long as couple of paragraphs. And every associate should be able to memorize and recite it.

For instance, the Ritz-Carlton Hotel Group has a classic vision statement:

Ladies and gentlemen serving ladies and gentlemen.

At our restaurant, this was our vision statement:

To create a place that pleases people.

A leader's vision should make the wildest dream seem achievable. A leader's vision is the organization's target. It's embodied in the mission statement and echoed in the employee handbook. The vision supports the entire corporate culture. It's the leader's responsibility to create a strong vision that works for everybody.

History has taught us that a shared vision is power. Circa 500 B.C., Aesop wrote in his fable, "The Bundle of Sticks," that it's easy to break a single stick, but impossible to break a bundle of them.

> *If you are of one mind and unite to assist each other, you will be as this bundle, uninjured by all the attempts of your enemies; but if you are divided among yourselves, you will be broken as easily as these sticks.*

Just as a group is stronger than an individual, a shared vision with shared values can help you reach a more powerful outcome than working alone to achieve your goals.

The men and women whose visions gave us Disneyland, Velcro®, and home delivery pizza must have initially seemed crazy. Nevertheless, their 20/20 visions held up against the scrutiny of all the naysayers and pessimists who couldn't see the world as they saw it. With vision must come the courage to believe in it and the passion to instill it in others.

I have always been intrigued by the word "supervision." It is a compound word used synonymously with "leadership" and encapsulates the most unique quality found in true leaders…Super-Vision.

Genuine Leader

Sol Price, the founder of Price Club – the first major warehouse club – had a great vision and the courage to follow it through. Imagine being a fly on the wall when he pitched his new business model to his first investors. The idea might have sounded like this:

"I'm proposing to build an entirely new retail concept that will use large buildings with concrete floors and open ceilings in remote locations where the land is less expensive. I envision a store with virtually no décor or amenities. It will be stocked with only 3500 items (compared to 35,000 in a typical grocery store). Many products will be one-time-buys, which will build a perception of scarcity and thereby create a greater sense of purchase urgency. Most of the products will be sold in commercial bulk packs like those used by restaurants. The concept I'm thinking about must have a very low payroll and therefore almost no customer service. Because of these spartan characteristics, we'll be able to offer very low prices. And by the way, I'm anticipating charging an annual fee for the privilege of shopping there."

With all these negatives offset by only one positive (low price), it's amazing that Sol Price ever got his concept off the ground. His compelling vision and personal motivation made it happen. Price Club's investors had to believe the leader's vision.

A clear vision is essential to any successful endeavor; however, if that vision is based on ill-conceived theories or baseless reasoning, it's doomed to failure. Furthermore, as much as a visionary must have passion, all the enthusiasm in the world won't help a flawed thesis or an uneducated premise become successful. As a popular bumper sticker puts it, "No Guts? No Glory! No Brains? Same Story!"

There's no substitute for being smart. You need to know the answers – or be smart enough to find the answers – to the challenges that you'll face. And a laundry list of college degrees won't necessarily provide you with the smarts that you need. The alumni lists of universities contain many corporate failures. At the same time, we all know about Bill Gates, Steve Jobs, Ted Turner, Michael Dell, and many other business leaders who dropped out of college so that they could pursue their visions.

The business smarts that you need include being rational, reasonable, and competent. Also, you need the will and desire to research, learn, and keep learning. It would be crazy to pursue a vision without investigating the pertinent facts. For example, if you had a vision to open a designer umbrella store in Las Vegas, where they experience less than five inches of rain a year, instead of in Tallahassee, where residents are annually drenched with over 65 inches, your visionary enthusiasm would be based on poor reasoning and would have a low probability of success.

Pretenders react to intuition, hunches, and transitory trends without doing the work necessary to validate their ideas. Genuine Leaders know that they must always be smart. When smart meets a clear vision, great things can happen.

Question 4. Where are we going?

A mission statement is your organization's road map. It spells out the organization's strategic initiatives in broad terms. The mission statement embodies the leader's vision and communicates the organization's reason for existing.

Anheuser-Busch, maker of Budweiser beer, has a very clear mission:
Be the world's beer company;
enrich and entertain a global audience;
deliver superior returns to our shareholders.

I carefully worded my mission statement for my restaurant to incorporate the many key elements of a food service enterprise:
To Provide All Guests with the Uniquely Satisfying Experience of Having Great Food and Fabulous Ice Cream, Served Expeditiously, in an

Unquestionably Clean, Safe, and Promotionally Exciting Restaurant, by Folks Who Genuinely Enjoy Being Around Other Folks...100% of the Time!

I saw how our mission statement effectively guided our organization many times, as the following two examples illustrate.

One day, I watched Mark, a server, walk over a straw wrapper twice while I was talking with a guest. On his third pass over the straw wrapper, I asked him to please pick it up. As he stooped to pick up the wrapper, he said, "Oops, sorry!" A fellow server, Jennifer, witnessed the interaction. As she passed Mark, she recited a portion of our mission statement: "...in an unquestionably clean and safe and promotionally exciting restaurant." I was pleasantly surprised by her verbatim recitation and was proud of the way she took our abstract mission statement and applied it to the situation at hand. I rewarded her on the spot with a grateful handshake and a $20 bill.

The second story came out of one of my T.E.A.M. Meetings (Thoughts Exchanged by Associates and Management). This bi-monthly discussion session was an opportunity for my associates and me to talk about any issues that had come up in the store. During this particular meeting, my associate Shannon asked why we had smoking sections when our mission statement contained the phrase "in an unquestionably clean and safe restaurant." My answer was that all 20 of our immediate competitors offered smoking sections. She countered that explanation, saying, "But our mission statement seems to prohibit it."

I was speechless for several seconds before I confessed that she was correct. What we were doing operationally obviously contradicted our mission statement. I then promised her that within three months, I would either eliminate the smoking sections or rewrite our mission statement.

Two months later, I abolished smoking in our two existing restaurants and opened our third restaurant as a completely smoke-free environment. Customer support was more favorable than I'd anticipated, and my associates were thrilled. With our mission statement, an 18-year-old part-time server was able to guide our organization in the right direction when I, the president, had led it astray.

A mission statement must not be static; rather, it needs to be able to evolve in accordance with the needs of the company. As I entered one of our restaurants in the late afternoon one day, Tanya, a relatively new greeter, intercepted me. She looked uncharacteristically concerned and asked to discuss an incident with me that had really bothered her. "Something just happened that I don't think you want in our restaurant," she said. That really got my attention. Her use of the phrase "our restaurant" moved me to take immediate action, so I invited her to join me in a quieter corner of the lobby.

Tanya proceeded to tell me that David, a Caucasian server, had just told Tanya, an African-American, not to seat any more "ghetto tables" in his section. Stunned, I asked Tanya to repeat the entire story, word for word, being careful not to leave out any details and without embellishing the facts. I warned her that what she said would likely result in either David's termination on grounds of racism or her own termination on grounds of false accusation.

With unflinching poise and complete confidence, Tanya repeated her story without varying one word or inflection. I thanked her profusely for her courage and trust and asked her to return to her reception podium. I assured her that I would take care of the situation immediately.

My manager saw me speaking with Tanya and respectfully waited for her to go back to her post before asking me what had happened. Within 10 minutes, she had found other servers to take over David's four tables so I could speak to him in the same corner of the lobby. I wanted Tanya and the others to see me talking to David.

As David approached, he seemed unable to make eye contact, which was unusual for the normally gregarious server. Without much introduction, I bluntly asked him about the "ghetto tables" request. His response was instantaneous and damning: "Yes, I said it, but I didn't mean anything racial by it." I knew right away why Tanya was so upset. She knew that "our restaurant" had zero tolerance for such behavior.

I physically removed the nametag from David's shirt and terminated him on the spot. Additionally, I banned him and any of his friends or relatives who shared his racial bias from the premises forever. I told him that we would mail him his last paycheck, and I escorted him out the front door.

It may have been just my imagination, but I think that our team got stronger that day. I know that the situation helped define more clearly the type of business we wanted to operate.

That evening, I reviewed our mission statement to see what went wrong (hiring someone like David) and what went right (earning Tanya's respect and confidence). Our original mission statement began with the following phrase: "To provide our guests…"

Then it dawned on me that one crucial word was missing: "all". Our subsequently rewritten mission statement began, "To provide all our guests." By adding the word "all" to the opening line, we closed a loophole that bigots like David might have used in the future to discriminate between the type of guests they wanted to serve and those they didn't. Thanks to Tanya, our mission became clearer and the organization became stronger.

Question 5. How are we going to get there?

Leaders and managers within an organization use *strategic* plans with carefully detailed goals to execute their mission. These plans are shared with every member of the organization. Planning and goal writing will be thoroughly described in Chapter Two.

Question 6. What needs to get done, and when do we begin?

These questions are answered in to-do lists drafted by leaders. To-do lists are written for the achievement of short, medium, and long-term goals that will keep the organization moving toward the full realization of its mission.

Addressing these Six Questions is a major step in the development of a solid organization. The answers provide a clear direction for Genuine Leaders, managers, and all participants.

The Culture Equation: How it All Comes Together

$$(sV+Vs+MS)P=C$$

You can represent how a culture is created by using the following formula:

The Variables:	Shared Values	=	sV
	Vision Statement	=	Vs
	Mission Statement	=	Ms
	Leader's Passion	=	P
	Company Culture	=	C

The Equation:	(sV + Vs + Ms) P	=	C

This equation represents what happens when you add the Shared Values (sV), the Vision Statement (Vs), and Mission Statement (Ms) together, then multiply this sum by the leader's positive presence or Passion (P). This equation clearly demonstrates the magnitude of the leader's influence on creating an organization's culture.

Your Culture and Your Bottom Line

What does the term "corporate culture" really mean? Many think of corporate culture as the indeterminate soft side of business, not directly connected to the mathematics underlying the organization's bottom line. Nothing could be further from the truth. In fact, the corporate culture is the spinal column of the business; the entire corporate body is structured around it.

In the July 17, 2006 edition of *Nation's Restaurant News*, Stephen J. Caldeira and Louise van der Does address the importance of a strong corporate culture. They define corporate culture as "…a company's shared values, beliefs and behavioral norms. It's a shared understanding of assumptions and expectations among an organization's members, and it is reflected in the policies, vision and goals of that organization." The authors demonstrate that cultural traits such as "involvement, consistency, adaptability and mission" are directly linked to performance measures, "…including return on investment, product development, sales growth, market share, quality and employee satisfaction."

Caldeira and Van der Does refer to several recent studies that also demonstrate the validity of linking corporate culture with financial success. One study of 950 businesses found that companies with excellent culture scores had a 21% return on equity, while those with exceptionally low culture scores posted a 6% return on equity. Researchers at Harvard Business School studied 10 companies in each of 20 different industries. Their report stated that when they found a strong corporate culture, revenues grew four times faster, there were seven times more jobs created, stock prices rose 12 times faster, and overall profits were 750% higher!

PASS-I-ON

In order to motivate and energize associates about a vision, the leader must have passion. The word "passion" can be dissected into three parts: PASS-I-ON. The leader needs to PASS his/her (I) vision, goals, and enthusiasm ON to others so that the dream can become a reality.

> ## Nothing great in the world
> ## has ever been accomplished without passion.
> *George Frederick Hegel, German philosopher*

What if Sol Price hadn't had passion when passing his vision on? We might never have known the exhilaration of warehouse shopping with huge shopping carts and small prices. What if Mary Kay Ash hadn't been able to energize thousands of women to take cosmetic sales door-to-door, inspiring them with her passion? What if Debbi Fields hadn't had the vision and passion to convince others that home-baked cookies could be sold in shopping malls?

Luck and timing undoubtedly play important roles in any successful enterprise, but a visionary's passion is at the root of just about every success story. Genuine Leaders skillfully pass their vision on to their associates through their passion.

People with "magnetic" and "charismatic" personalities are all driven by passion. You've undoubtedly been influenced by someone's passion many times throughout your life. Consider a vacation tour guide who says, "Let's go white water rafting tomorrow afternoon – it's the greatest feeling in the world! It's such a thrill!" You'd probably be eager to go.

But think about a guide who says, "We offer white water rafting, but it's pricey and it takes all afternoon. Also, it can be dangerous, and you'll definitely get soaked." You'd probably find an excuse to stay behind. Genuine Leaders inspire with their passion, while Pretenders distance themselves from their associates with their ho-hum demeanor.

Passion is to a vision
As oxygen is to a fire…
A little gets it started,
A continuous source keeps it glowing.

Genuine Leader

The 70% Passion Test

If you're like me, you've met dozens of irresponsible managers and Pretenders who seem disengaged or ambivalent about the work they do. We hear them say, "Some days are better than others…hey, it's a job…the work's steady…it's a paycheck," and so on.

This lackadaisical attitude towards an activity that takes up such a major portion of your life has always befuddled me. If you didn't like your work, why wouldn't you leave and find something else to do? Why would you just accept whatever was handed to you as long as a large enough paycheck was attached?

Nowadays, we're seeing lots of business professionals quit their six-figure incomes to run a bed and breakfast or a hardware store in a small city. People are beginning to understand that passion for what they're doing is more important in the long run than an extra digit on their paycheck.

**An average Leader looks forward to going to work
at least 70% of the time. Genuine leaders—at least 90%.**

If you've ever wondered if you're in the right job, take my 70% Passion Test. To apply my test, take a 10-day period and record the number of mornings that you wake up and truly look forward to going to work. Don't think about how you feel when the alarm first goes off or when you can't find a matching pair of socks. Wait until after you're dressed and ready to face the day. Then ask yourself, "Am I really looking forward to going to work?"

The 70% Passion Test states that if you can't offer an emphatic "yes" to this question on seven out of 10 days, you, and by extension the people around you, have a huge problem. You have a problem because your life will become more and more miserable. Your co-workers have a problem because they won't be looking forward to seeing you each morning. The rationale that "I may hate the job, but the money is good," doesn't hold up for long. Your negative attitude will cause both your business and your personal life to turn sour. The "good money" will evaporate fast in divorce court, and the health ailments caused by your attitudinal malaise are very real.

Think of the last time you went home early from work. Was your family thrilled to see you? Or did they immediately whine, "Why are you home so early? We weren't expecting you until later." If you love what you do at least 70% of the time, the pleasure you get out of your job will transfer to your personal life. But if you're always in a bad mood, your family will cringe when they hear your car pull into the driveway.

Here's another quick test. What happened the last time you told your staff about your upcoming vacation? Did they seem more excited about it than you? And when you told them that the vacation would last two full weeks, did they give each other high-fives in the break room? If you love what you do at least 70% of the time, your presence in the workplace will be missed instead of applauded. And if you don't, your people will fantasize about your next vacation before you get back from this one.

A great leader's courage to fulfill his vision comes from passion, not position.

John Maxwell, American author and speaker

What To Do?

Craig and his wife Jill were business partners who asked to speak with me privately after a seminar. They described their business to me in great detail. They

had invested five years of their life and all of their money in a business that catered to a specific niche market, and they were having a difficult time making it work.

When they finished, I asked them three questions:

➥ Have you attempted to learn the language of the people you are trying to serve?

➥ Do you hold regular meetings with your associates, and have you conducted focus group sessions with your prospective customers to learn more about their needs and wants?

➥ Do you wake up in the morning looking forward to going to work at least 70% of the time?

After hearing "no" to the first two questions, I had an idea about what their answer to number three would be. As I awaited their response, I was touched by the look they exchanged. A look that spoke volumes about their last five years. They each struggled to say "yes," but instead they offered a resounding "no!"

Immediately I said, "You should sell your business to the highest bidder as soon as possible." Their relief was palpable. They reacted as if I had just released them from their chains. The 70% Passion Test helped them to see what had been right under their noses the whole time.

Now it's your turn. Apply the 70% Test to your job. If you score 70% or higher, great! If you score lower than 70%, please begin to look for something else to do with your life. Take whatever's left of your positive attitude to some other endeavor. The "good money" will follow.

I believe a person needs just three things to be truly happy in this world: someone or something to love, something meaningful to do, and something to look forward to. The 70% Passion Test should help you determine if you're fortunate enough to have found any or all of these in your job.

If you are not fired with enthusiasm, you will be fired with enthusiasm.

Vince Lombardi, football coach

Passionate leaders feel pain when they're involved in an initiative that results in anything less than success. They're reluctant to stop at "good enough." They anguish over leaving something "on the field" or "in the tank." They crave the endorphin release they feel when they give their all to the job at hand. Have you ever noticed how people's actions are different after a major initiative that taxes the entire organization both physically and mentally? Typically, the associates and managers are exhausted, but the leaders are exhilarated.

You've got passion if you "tingle" before handling a meaningful task or an important project. Passion is the adrenaline rush you get during an assignment and the euphoria you feel after its successful completion. Additionally, a passionate person feels a greater sense of remorse when they know that something could have been done better. A dispassionate leader will simply shrug and walk away.

> Actually, there is very little difference in people, but that little difference makes a big difference. The little difference is attitude. The big difference is whether it is positive or negative.
>
> W. Clement Stone, American businessman

Passion is a "We Can Do This!" Attitude

Passion separates the memorable leaders from the mediocre. It's the quality that most effectively influences others. Passionate leaders achieve far greater goals than a dispassionate leader could ever imagine. A shy, solemn, or sedentary Pretender will struggle fruitlessly to achieve greatness. An outgoing, upbeat, and involved Genuine Leader inspires the team to work doubly hard so that they can realize their vision.

Former British Prime Minister Margaret Thatcher defined success as a combination of the following:

1. "Having a sense of purpose" (your *vision*)
2. "Having a flair for what you are doing" (your *passion*)
3. "Hard work" (your *character*)

SUMMARY SCORE: *Benchmarking Your Ability to Lead*

At the end of each chapter, I'll ask you to make a personal evaluation of your current performance level with regard to the topic we've discussed – in this case, your Vision and your Passion for what you do.

Grade yourself using a 1-10 scale. Keep in mind that a 1 doesn't signify an utter failure and 10 doesn't mean perfection. It's essential that you use the entire 1-10 scale as thoughtfully as possible. At the end of the book, you'll add up your scores, creating a quantified assessment of your ability to lead. More importantly, these numbers will also serve as your benchmarks from which you'll be able to measure your future progress.

Are you a passionate leader with 20/20 vision? What would be an accurate assessment of your ability to develop a meaningful vision and to promote it passionately?

Score yourself on a scale of 1-10

Recommendations to Raise Your *Vision and Passion* Score:

1. Conduct an associate attitude survey annually.

Make sure that your survey contains questions that will assess the effectiveness of your mission statement. In your survey, you might want to use statements like the samples below, using this response key: Strongly Agree, Agree, Disagree, or Strongly Disagree.

a. "Our company has a mission statement we refer to often."

b. "The top management has a clear view of where we are going as a company."

c. "It is clear to me and to the general public what our company stands for."

2. Tell interesting stories about how your business got started.

You can do this at any of your group meetings. Many people dream of starting their own business someday, and they're interested in how the organization came into being. As the stories become more familiar, the team will begin to feel like they've been involved since day one.

3. Challenge your people to learn your values and mission statements "by heart."

Begin each and every meeting with a group recitation of the statements, or choose a volunteer to recite them. The more often the phrases are repeated, the more likely your associates will understand and live by them. When walking around the company, don't ask general questions such as "How's business?" or "Is everything going okay?" Instead, ask, "What goal are you working toward?" or "Are we living our values today?"

4. Connect your message to the mission statement whenever possible.

For example, you can say, "Stacy, would you please call the customer and ask if she would like us to deliver the item that we inadvertently left out of her order? Our mission statement promises 'unsurpassed service,' and we want to live up to that promise." This will remind Stacy that the mission statement's purpose is to guide the daily activities of all levels of the business.

5. Assess your passion level.

Now that you know what passion is, let's try to measure yours with the following Passion Assessment exercise. It's more detailed than the quick 70% Passion Test. These 30 questions are centered on activities that passionate leaders engage in regularly. Read over each question and determine the frequency with which you perform it or a similar activity, and score yourself accordingly.

When you've got your answers, use our scoring guide to determine your passion level. The most important aspect of this test is not your grade – it's the 30 examples of how you might showcase your passion every day.

PASSION...WHAT'S LEFT OF YOURS?

	3 Recently	2 A while ago	1 Can't remember the last time	0 Maybe never
When was the last time you...				
1. **Called the manager** in charge of the late shift to ask how the night went and to acknowledge how much you appreciate his/her efforts?	____	____	____	____
2. **Sat and listened** to an 18-year-old employee tell you about his/her complex young life?	____	____	____	____
3. **Spoke with a vendor** to ask about the hottest new marketing idea he/she has seen recently?	____	____	____	____

	3	2	1	0
	Recently	A while ago	Can't remember the last time	Maybe never

4. **Conducted a performance review** that was thoroughly prepared, professionally enlightening, and emotionally supportive? .... ____   ____   ____   ____

5. **Said "please" and "thank you"** after requesting something from one of your employees? .... ____   ____   ____   ____

6. **Held a meeting** with 10 or more employees (and no managers) for 60-90 minutes to determine whether or not they liked their jobs and the people they work with? .... ____   ____   ____   ____

7. **Asked one of your associates,** "How are you?" and really listened to the response? .... ____   ____   ____   ____

8. **Read a good book** and then bought copies for your managers so they could share the experience? .... ____   ____   ____   ____

9. **Took your key players** away for a day (or two) of fun and fellowship without worrying how the business would look the next day? .... ____   ____   ____   ____

10. **Laughed** uncontrollably with a group of employees? .... ____   ____   ____   ____

11. **Called a "long-termer"** (15+ years) at home out of the blue and told him/her how much you appreciate your relationship? .... ____   ____   ____   ____

12. **Thanked a vendor** for his/her professionalism and dedication to serving your business? .... ____   ____   ____   ____

13. **Sent a personally written note** of thanks to the home of an associate who went out of his/her way to satisfy a customer or to make your business better? .... ____   ____   ____   ____

14. **Personally tried to use a piece of equipment** that everyone has been complaining about – and then replaced it? .... ____   ____   ____   ____

15. **Helped your managers achieve a better balance** between their lives at home and at work? ____   ____   ____   ____

	3 Recently	2 A while ago	1 Can't remember the last time	0 Maybe never
16. **Referred to part-timers as "prime-timers"** in words and spirit?	___	___	___	___
17. **Took a call from an irate customer** because you wanted to offer overwhelming empathy that would lead to a complete recovery?	___	___	___	___
18. **Apologized to an associate** and admitted that you were wrong?	___	___	___	___
19. **"Worked as a clerk"** for an entire day just to put your feet in your employees' shoes?	___	___	___	___
20. **Held a lottery for your staff** for two free tickets to an incredible event that were given to you by a supplier?	___	___	___	___
21. **"Took the hit"** instead of blaming the corporate office for a major snafu?	___	___	___	___
22. **Wrote a personal letter of thanks** to a deserving associate at least two levels below you on the organizational chart simply to say, "Thanks for the great job you do"?	___	___	___	___
23. **Drew a smiley face on a scrap of paper** and tucked it into a stack of work for your assistant to find later?	___	___	___	___
24. **Slept seven consecutive hours** for seven consecutive nights?	___	___	___	___
25. **Attended a department level meeting** to hear the latest issues in that department?	___	___	___	___
26. **Removed a harshly-worded memo** that a manager had posted on the employees' bulletin board?	___	___	___	___
27. **Called a new employee at home** to ask if he/she is enjoying the new job?	___	___	___	___
28. **Sat with a new employee** at lunch to evaluate your orientation program from his/her perspective?	___	___	___	___

	3 *Recently*	**2** *A while ago*	**1** *Can't remember the last time*	**0** *Maybe never*
29. **Sent a letter to each of your associates at home** to thank them for their great effort over the past 12 months and to outline your company's strategic focus during the next year?....	____	____	____	____
30. **Really looked forward to returning to work** after a great vacation?	____	____	____	____

Scoring:

60 + ...Your passion is a beacon of light

45 – 59 ....Your passion continues to burn

30 – 44 ....There remains a flicker of hope

29 or less ....Your batteries are low

Your Total = _____

RECOMMENDED READING

➡ The Leadership Challenge
by Jim M. Kouzes and Barry Z. Posner *(Jossey-Bass, 2003)*

➡ The Passion Plan at Work: A Step-by-Step Guide to Building a Passion-Driven Organization
by Richard Y. Chang *(Jossey-Bass, 2001)*

➡ More Than a Pink Cadillac: Mary Kay Inc.'s Nine Leadership Keys to Success
by Jim Underwood *(McGraw-Hill, 2004)*

➡ Little Gold Book of YES! Attitude: How to Find, Build and Keep a YES! Attitude for a Lifetime of SUCCESS
by Jeffrey Gitomer *(FT Press, 2006)*

CHAPTER 2

GENUINE LEADERS CREATE, PLAN, AND EXECUTE

Your problem is to bridge
the gap that exists
between where you are now
and the goal
you intend to reach.

Earl Nightingale, American motivational speaker

The Trifecta

Leaders get things done in three distinct, sequential, and inseparable phases.

In the **Creative Phase**, the Genuine Leader brainstorms many ideas to solve a problem or answer a question.

In the **Planning Phase**, the Genuine Leader organizes the available resources and develops a plan to set the idea in motion.

And in the **Execution Phase**, the Genuine Leader executes goals in a timely manner to successfully complete the initiative.

It's not enough to be skilled in only one or two of these phases. An incredible idea without a PLAN is nothing more than a daydream. A great plan without EXECUTION is nothing more than meaningless words. Pretenders may be accomplished in one or two of these phases, but Genuine Leaders have the skills that enable them to complete the Trifecta: to Create, Plan, and Execute. Instead of trying to solve today's problems with yesterday's solutions, they come up with new answers. They don't let great ideas wither on the vine. They develop an action plan and see it through to the end.

PHASE 1 – CREATING IDEAS AND SOLUTIONS

Thinking
is the hardest work there is,
which is probably the reason so few engage in it.

Henry Ford, American industrialist

What is Creativity?

Here's how neuroscientist Nancy Andreasen defines creativity:

> *Creativity is a process that starts with a person who's trying to figure out a better way of doing a task at work or at home. That person must think about their problem or their project in a novel way and then come up with a solution. The creative process can go by in a flash or it can take years. But the end result is the production of something new and useful, such as the automobile, or beautiful, such as a painting by Vincent Van Gogh.*
>
> *No one knows for sure how the brain produces creativity, but research suggests that creative people often slip into a zone in which ideas and thoughts come up freely in a disorganized way. During that state, a part of the brain known as the association cortex becomes very active. The brain region is known to be able to link up ideas or thoughts in potentially novel ways.*

It's not just writers, musicians, and artists who are creative. In the business world, there are countless examples of creativity: new products, novel approaches to distribution, new slants on product use, etc. Every one of us has the potential to rock the world – or at least our little corner of it – with a creative idea.

Think Outside Your Box

Creativity allows a Genuine Leader to think outside the box. You can't do the same thing over and over again and expect different results. Creativity allows us to think in new directions. A business associate, Roger L. Smith, told me that you can either "think outside the box or be buried in one by the competition."

H-E-B, with headquarters in San Antonio, Texas, is one of the food industry leaders. Their creativity and level of execution is legendary in food retailing. Just a quick look at their website (www.heb.com) will show you how they differ from their competitors.

I was fortunate enough to witness their brilliance up close during a few of their management conferences. On one occasion, I asked a senior store manager how H-E-B manages to create the many new merchandising and marketing innovations that allow them to stay ahead of the competition.

"Pressure," he responded.

"Pressure to what?" I asked.

He said, "Pressure to spend 60% of our time on the job changing the business and 40% of our time running the business. In contrast, in my previous job with another company, we spent 100% of our time running the business." H-E-B's ratio was one of the most profound business values I've ever heard. It's a blueprint for staying on top. H-E-B's corporate commitment to embrace change and to avoid complacency is carried straight down through all levels of the business. The emphasis on imagination and creativity is one of the major reasons why H-E-B's average store volume is over two times higher than the industry average.

You can't wait for inspiration. You have to go after it with a club.

Jack London, American author

Creativity transforms a soft-edged vision into a hard-lined mission statement and a mission statement into a viable strategic plan. You or I might have thought about a market for next-day delivery of letters and packages, but only Frederick W. Smith had the creative genius to take that idea, which started as a C- term paper he wrote for a college economics course, and turn it into Federal Express.

Most of us have spent time in a coffee shop, but only Howard Schultz envisioned how he could take a few little coffee shops in Seattle and turn them into Starbucks, the iconic mega-chain.

We have all been frustrated at one time or another because we didn't have access to duplicating machines or computers, but it took Paul Orfalea to channel that aggravation into Kinko's Copies, which now has franchises located near almost every college campus and major urban center in the country.

PHASE 2 – PLANNING THE IDEA OR SOLUTION

If you employed study, thinking, and planning time daily, you could develop and use the power that can change the course of your destiny.

W. Clement Stone, American businessman

Landing a man on the moon had been our nation's dream for generations, but it wasn't until President John F. Kennedy put a plan into place that we accomplished this incredible feat. Millions of brilliant ideas have failed to take off because they haven't had a plan behind them. The time-consuming planning process is what brings the idea off the drawing board and into reality.

An ancient Chinese proverb says, "A journey of a thousand miles must begin with a single step." Thousands of years later, Mark Twain wrote, "The secret of getting ahead is getting started. The secret of getting started is breaking your complex, overwhelming tasks into small manageable tasks and then starting on the first one." Planning is the process of dissecting a larger vision into small, distinct steps. A carefully-crafted strategic plan that is broken into bite-size tasks inspires and motivates everyone involved.

A strategic plan's purpose is to eliminate the unknowns, minimize the uncertainties, and increase predictability. If outcomes can be made more predictable, the probability of success increases. Remember: Failing to Plan Is a Plan to Fail.

A key component to any successful plan is its ability to be measured. If you are going to be able to manage anything, you must be able to measure the multiple steps along the way. And if you're going to be able to measure these steps, you must fully define the work needed to complete each of them. This measurement process is sometimes referred to as task analysis. Each mini-task has to be able to be measured appropriately so you can ensure that it is generating the desired results.

A baseball coach's vision of winning his team's division might begin with the mini-task of raising the team's batting average by 25 points. To achieve this goal, the coach could increase each batting practice by 30 minutes, add one additional practice per week, and hire a sports psychologist for those in need.

In order to create an effective plan, a leader must be able to focus on it. Benjamin Franklin understood the necessity of concentration:

> *I have always thought that one man of tolerable abilities may work great changes and accomplish great affairs among mankind, if he first forms a good plan, and cutting off all amusements or other employments that would divert his attention, make the execution of that same plan his sole study and business.*

Staying the course, maintaining focus, and avoiding pitfalls are needed to pull off a successful plan. For instance, organizing a marathon race for charity can be a huge undertaking, so a strategic plan is an absolute must. A few years ago, a Category Two hurricane blew through a planned race venue in Virginia Beach. Although most people would have thrown in the towel, the focused planning that had gone into the race allowed the organizers to still have a successful event against all odds.

A plan is a predetermined course of action to achieve specific results within a stated period of time. Proper planning necessitates the ability to focus on the details of a project without losing sight of the overall objective. You have to be able to see both the forest and the trees simultaneously.

In general terms, the planning process entails the following steps:

✓ Gathering information on the topics involved in the plan

✓ Considering future conditions, both external and internal, and forecasting accordingly

✓ Lining up the staffing, material, and capital resources necessary to achieve the ultimate objective

✓ Breaking down your objective into smaller operational tasks and assigning the proper people to them

Let's take a sample objective and see how we might break it into smaller tasks.

Objective: To reduce the turnover of newly-hired associates by 10% in 12 months.

Our main **Goal** might be to improve the orientation process of all new employees. The goal would then be broken into several tasks spread out over time.

Task 1 might be to interview 50 newly-hired associates to determine their opinion of the orientation that they received.

Task 2 might be to increase the amount of orientation time each new associate would receive by five hours.

Task 3 might be to create a new "Welcome" video that would include a message from the company's president outlining the organization's mission statement.

Task 4 might be to institute a buddy system that would assign a more experienced associate to accompany a new employee on breaks and lunches during his or her first 30 days.

Task 5 might be identifying a method of measuring the new associate's progress.

Five or six tasks could be sufficient to complete this plan. But be willing to take all the necessary actions you need. This is no place for shortcuts. The train to success is not an express – it's a local that requires many stops along the way.

The measurement mechanisms used to determine the success of the objective that we outlined above could include measuring the percentage change in annual employee turnover or measuring the change in the attitude surveys from associates from year to year.

Why Bother to Plan? After All...

One complaint about the planning process that I often hear is, "Why bother? After all, so many uncontrollable factors impact our organization that our final draft of the plan could be rendered useless the moment it's written."

There are two obvious reasons for investing time in the planning process. First, plans allow us to execute our work and our goals more efficiently. Second, plans allow us to be better prepared for change. If Plan A is stalled by weather, competition, the economy, etc., we can fall back onto a pre-conceived Plan B.

There are at least two additional, albeit less obvious, benefits to planning. First, it's a great team-building activity. During the planning process, the individuals involved learn more about each other and how they fit into the company's overall mission. Sometimes the actual strategic document that is created is less valuable than the communication and camaraderie generated during the process.

Second, the skill sets learned during the planning process can be carried over to other management activities. Brainstorming, compromising, and forming action plans are extremely useful and necessary abilities for many aspects of any business.

Preparing for New Competition

What do we do when a new competitor comes to town? Theoretically, our leadership instincts should go into overdrive. We should attempt to develop a plan that will allow us to retain our market share and our existing associates. Pretenders will often adopt a wait-and-see policy, ignoring the newcomer and hoping that their customers will magically remain loyal. Genuine Leaders, on the other hand, prepare for battle the moment that the rumor of an incursion becomes a reality. They realize that if you're forced to make radical changes prior to the entry of a new competitor, it's probably too late. Your plan of action must be in place long before the competitor's opening, and your major adjustments should be installed months in advance.

Jeff Noddle, the chairman of the food wholesaler/retailer SUPERVALU, emphasizes that a leader should have a "healthy dose of paranoia." He says that being paranoid with respect to your market share and competitive incursions will force you to operate with a plan and backup options.

My first serious competitive attack came from a regional discount department store. I was managing a large shopping center, and I'd anticipated the competitor's inevitable arrival because we had been carefully tracking its rapidly expanding domain. With 18 months' notice to prepare, we felt like we were in control of our destiny.

In the first 12 months, we aggressively worked to improve our internal deficiencies, such as human resource issues that might have caused associate defections to our new neighbor, something I wanted to avoid at all costs. We embarked on a facility remodeling program to freshen up our appearance, and we sped up plans to upgrade our point-of-sale technology.

In the last three months before the competitor opened its doors, we developed a full marketing and advertising plan to prepare for the competition. We had collected several grand opening advertisements from the new chain's other recent openings so we could identify some marketing strategies and sale items that they might use against us.

In the end, we were scared but prepared. This regional powerhouse was on a march. Their momentum was unnerving. And their selection of a site that was literally next door to us showed that they were clearly after our market share.

From the look of their parking lot on opening day, their kickoff was obviously a huge success. I had to suppress thoughts of doing immature things to their customers' cars that had parked in our lot due to our new neighbor's overflow reception.

We kept our fingers crossed as we rolled out our marketing strategy to bring our customers back. Part of the plan included a one-time, four-course, 19¢ chicken dinner, which we served to thousands in our parking lot during the competitor's opening day. We ran a double-truck ad for two weeks with the headline "Welcome Our New Neighbors," listing over 50 items that they would probably run against us. Due to their size and printing lead times, they were unable to change their ad, and they looked rather foolish when they advertised items that we had sold two weeks earlier at lower prices.

Happily for us, their opening month was less successful than they'd anticipated. When I finally got the courage to walk through their big, beautiful store, I heard two announcements over the intercom that suggested our strategic plan wasn't the only thing hurting their opening. They seemed to be self-destructing from the start. The two public address announcements that I heard were:

1. "Attention shoppers, please look after your kids. The store is really busy and we are not about to send our employees around to look for them." (Did I hear that right?)

2. "Due to the local fire ordinance, smoking is not allowed in this store." (In fact, no such ordinance existed at that time.)

We soon discovered that the first impression our new neighbor was projecting was that of a rude and unhelpful store. Also, the fact that they had lied about an ordinance to stop people from smoking in the store didn't help them win their customers' affection. With these missteps, it wasn't too long before the competitor had closed their doors and moved on. Our creative planning and counterattack promotions, combined with their self-destructive tendencies, facilitated the competitor's early demise.

PHASE 3 – EXECUTING THE PLAN

Everyone who's ever taken a shower has an idea.
It's the person who gets out of the shower,
dries off, and does something about it
who makes a difference.

Nolan Bushnell, founder of Atari

Most companies don't fail for lack of talent or strategic vision – they fail due to lack of execution. In sports and business alike, the level of execution separates the winners from the losers. Ultimately, we're judged by our results.

Exceptional execution happens when:

• **The objectives are clearly defined**, understood, and accepted by the people the plan affects.

• **The planned action is launched** in a timely manner by a decisive leader. There comes a time when it's necessary to stop talking and start doing. Two popular expressions, one from Larry the Cable Guy – "Git'er dun" – and the other from the Nike Corporation – "Just Do It" – sum up what needs to happen in the Execution Phase. Genuine Leaders don't make excuses and they don't lose their concentration.

• **The plan's progress is continuously evaluated**. The actual results are compared to the plan's expected performance.

• **Variations to the plan are analyzed** to determine the causes of any deviation.

• **Corrective adjustments to the plan** are made so that the desired results can be achieved. Hall of Fame football coach Don Shula called this process of adjustment "closing the gap" between what you say you're going to do and what you actually do.

Ray Kroc didn't invent McDonald's. He had discovered the single unit burger joint when he was a salesman selling paper supplies to the foodservice industry. But it was his vision for what McDonald's could become and his outstanding level of execution that enabled the concept to take off. John Mackey and his partners didn't invent the organic natural food store. But without their vision and level of execution, Whole Foods could easily have remained a small, local store like the many others that they eventually bought out.

Genuine Leaders take their vision and their plan far beyond what others see as possible. Their tenacity, perseverance, and plain old stick-to-itiveness allow them to go the distance. Genuine Leaders Create, Plan, and Execute.

Success seems to be largely a matter of hanging on after others have let go.

William Feather, American publisher and author

The Decision-Making Process

The following seven-step process, commonly taught in business school, is intended to help leaders creatively and methodically solve problems.

Step 1. Identify the real problem.

Step 2. Brainstorm all plausible solutions.

Step 3. Choose the two best alternatives.

Step 4. Create a plan for each of the two best alternatives.

Step 5. Implement the best alternative of the two (Plan A).

Step 6. Evaluate progress.

Step 7. Move to Plan B if Plan A fails.

Over the years, I've modified the seven steps a bit, but their spirit remains intact.

Let's look at how this valuable process uses a Genuine Leader's Creative, Planning, and Executing skills. For each step, I'll emphasize which of these three skill sets comes into play the most.

Step 1: Identify the REAL problem (CREATE)

In this step, you want to seek out the true cause of the problem, not just the most obvious reason it exists. An acquaintance in Thibodaux, Louisiana, likened this step to "finding the tick." As he described it to me, if your hound dog came in from outside and started to scratch himself incessantly, you might give him a nudge with your foot to make him stop. "Did you solve the problem?" he asked. "No. The dog simply moves away and goes about his scratching in another corner of the room. Now, let's say you go over to the dog and sprinkle some medicated powder on the rash you've discovered under his fur. Did you solve the problem? No, not yet. Next, you dig deep into his fur, find the bloated tick, and carefully remove it. Finally, you've solved the problem." Too many people think that the dog's superficial scratching is the problem. They accept the symptom as the issue and don't take the trouble to look deeper for the real cause of the itch.

In any situation, until you locate the "tick," you're only scratching the surface while wasting time, energy, and money.

Step 2: Brainstorm Potential Solutions (CREATE)

Whether your own brain does the "storming" or you use a committee of craniums, the purpose of this step is to come up with as many potential solutions to your project or problem as possible. Make sure that the flow of creative ideas is allowed free rein, and accept every idea without criticism. No idea is too "stupid" or "impractical." Write down everything, no matter how far-fetched it may seem at first hearing. Yesterday's nonsensical thought may be tweaked into tomorrow's brilliant plan.

After you've thoroughly exhausted the idea bank, you can move on to Step Three.

Step 3: Choose Two Potential Solutions (PLAN)

The leader then selects the two most plausible solutions from those listed during the brainstorming session and outlines a PLAN OF ACTION for each one. Who, What, Where, When, Why, and How issues need to be addressed in as much detail as possible. Two solutions are necessary because one will be the top pick and one will be the backup.

Step 4: Choose the best single alternative (PLAN)

Next, choose the one best plan that has the lowest risk and the highest reward potential. The other idea, Plan B, will be your fallback option.

Step 5: Implement the First Alternative (EXECUTE)

In this step, the plan is set into action. All responsible parties are assigned roles and put in place to execute the plan. If necessary, the leader makes adjustments to achieve maximum success.

Step 6: Evaluate results (EXECUTE)

The leader must evaluate the results of the plan at pre-determined checkpoints. If the results are meeting expectations, the plan is continued until the desired outcome is reached. IF NOT, and if there seems to be no way to get the plan back on track, we must move to the next step.

Step 7: Move to Plan B (EXECUTE)

When it becomes apparent that nothing is going to get Plan A moving forward, it's time to implement Plan B, the backup plan. To implement Plan B, go back to Step Five and continue the process again from there.

The Decision-Making Process in Action

When my company was developing our restaurant franchise agreement, we needed to find a location that would give us the best chance for success. After a six-month search and analysis process (Step 2), we identified four viable sites.

The business pro formas that we developed for each location identified two winners, and we recognized one site as a clear standout (Steps 3 and 4). Unfortunately, our preferred location was in an area with a slow zoning board that was notorious for an approval process that would take at least a year.

Since our development agreement with the franchisor would not allow such a delay, we quickly moved on to location B (Step 7), even though the profit projections for that site were not as favorable as those for location A. Having Plan B ready in the wings allowed us to move forward without missing a beat, and we could stay in compliance with our contractual obligations and our business plan. Incidentally, two years later, we acquired location A and were able to open there as well.

When choosing between two evils, I always like to try the one I've never tried before.

Mae West, actress

SUMMARY SCORE:

Are you a Genuine Leader who can Create, Plan, and Execute the actions necessary to design, build, and grow your project, department, or company?

Score yourself on a scale of 1-10

Recommendations to Raise Your *Create, Plan, and Execute* Score:

A. Raising your *Ability to CREATE* score:

1. **Keep a tape recorder or note pad near your bed and your shower.**

Curiously, ideas seem to flow in these environments. Capture them before they evaporate.

2. **Activate a suggestion box system.**

Talk up the process. Set aside time in your meetings to review the offerings and handsomely reward legitimate ideas.

3. **Expand your sources of ideas.**

For example, join or form an idea share group with others in your industry. The members should be from as geographically diverse an area as possible. I belonged to one such group for eight years, and it was my favorite source for new ideas and solutions to problems.

4. **Begin a Think Tank within your organization whose job is to generate new opportunities for growth and development.**

This group should meet at off-site venues that might stimulate thinking.

5. **Conduct customer and non-customer focus groups on a regular basis to explore new opportunities.**

6. **Learn to ask your people, "What do you think?"**

Too often, we shoot off an answer to an associate's question without seeking his or her solution first. You may find that the associate's suggestion will be as good or better than yours. By asking "What do you think?" I saved hours of brainstorming time, generated hundreds of new ideas, and made my associates feel much more involved, valuable, and appreciated.

7. **Give your team the Connect Test.**

In this classic "think outside the box" exercise, the objective is try to connect nine circles, first with four connecting straight lines, and again with three connecting straight lines, without lifting your pencil off the paper. This exercise is designed to encourage your associates to give their creative energies a workout. (You can find both solutions on our website: www.hlloydpresents.com.)

O O O
O O O
O O O

You can't run a business based on vague promises. "Weasel words" can confuse and derail a conversation or an entire project. An alert leader must step up and challenge a "weasel's" lack of commitment by asking the "weasel" to rephrase his/her statement more specifically.

The 10 Most Common "Weasel Words"	*Rewritten for Commitment*
1. I think I can	I know I will
2. I'll try to	I will do it by…
3. I hope to be done by	It will be complete by…
4. Maybe	Certainly
5. It's likely I'll	I'm sure I'll…
6. I ought to have it by	I'll have it no later than…
7. By the end of the week, okay?	Friday, 5:30 P.M.
8. Probably	Without a doubt
9. If all goes well I should	You can count on it by…
10. Sometime tomorrow	4:30 tomorrow

3. **Lead by example.** Leaders can't just preach the mission statement – they must execute it. If your associates see you cross the parking lot and step over a piece of litter, don't be disappointed when they don't keep their department clean. When you fail to smile and greet your employees, don't be surprised when you see them forget to appropriately acknowledge a customer.

4. **Share this poem with your team:**

Which Am I?

I watched them tear a building down;
A gang of men in a busy town.
With a mighty heave and lusty yell,
They swung a beam and a side wall fell.
I said to the foreman, "Are these men as skilled
As the men you'd hire if you had to build?"
He gave a laugh and said, "No indeed!
Just a common laborer is all I need.
And I can wreck in a day or two
What it took the builder a year to do."

8. Read *The Creating Brain: The Neuroscience of Genius,* in which Nanc Andreasen recommends ways to build a more creative brain.

For example, she suggests spending 30 minutes a day in a creativity workout doing one of the following:

- *Explore an unfamiliar area of knowledge.* For example, people who use a lot of math on the job could sign up for a painting or calligraphy class.
- *Spend time each day thinking.* Don't censor your thoughts, but allow your mind to go freely to a problem and see what solutions or ideas surface.
- *Practice the art of paying attention.* Look for a person or object in your daily commute that you hadn't noticed before and observe it closely. Try to describe or draw that object in a journal or sketchbook, or talk about it into a tape recorder.

B. Raising your *Ability to PLAN* score:

1. **Look at your regular meetings agenda.**

Analyze the amount of time you spend on future planning versus time spent debriefing the past. Do you allocate sufficient time to discuss tomorrow's business, or are you fixated on reviewing yesterday's results? My rule of thumb is that 25% of the time should be spent reviewing old business and updating progress on any existing business plan, and 75% of the agenda should be allocated to future events, issues, and plans.

2. **Schedule think time on your daily to-do list.**

I'm amazed at how many people in charge of important things don't allocate adequate quiet time to plan their ideas and projects. Many leaders resort to winging it, thereby drastically reducing the idea's chances for success.

3. **Involve as many capable people as possible.**

To increase the likelihood of a plan's success, be very thorough in explaining to your team why the plan is so important, and give as many associates as possible a role to play in the planning process. Their sense of ownership will power the process to a more successful conclusion.

C. Raising your *Ability to EXECUTE* Score:

1. **Always keep score of everything.**

Measure everything your unit does and share those results with your associates. Most people are more motivated by measured results than by subjective evaluations or empty praise.

2. **Avoid "weasel words."**

And I thought to myself as I went my way,
Just which of these roles have I tried to play?
Am I a builder who works with care
Creating things by the rule and square,
Or am I a wrecker as I walk the town
Content with the reputation of tearing down?

(Author Unknown)

5. Finally, remember what Yoda said in *Star Wars V : The Empire Strikes Back.* When Luke Skywalker was asked to raise his sunken Starfighter from the Dagobah swamps using only the power of his mind, he said that he would try. Yoda said to him, "Try not Luke! Do or do not. There is no try." I couldn't put it any better.

RECOMMENDED READING

➡ The Creating Brain: The Neuroscience of Genius
by Nancy Andreasen *(Dana Press, 2005)*

➡ Creativity Games for Trainers: A Handbook of Group Activities for Jumpstarting Workplace Creativity
by Robert Epstein *(McGraw-Hill, 1995)*

➡ A Whack on the Side of the Head: How You Can Be More Creative
by Roger Van Oech *(Business Plus, 1998)*

➡ Execution Plain and Simple: Twelve Steps to Achieving Any Goal On Time and On Budget
by Robert A. Nieman *(McGraw-Hill, 2004)*

➡ Execution: The Discipline of Getting Things Done
by Ram Charan and Larry Bossidy *(Crown Business, 2002)*

CHAPTER 3

A GENUINE LEADER IS AN EXCELLENT COMMUNICATOR

Communicate everything
you possibly can to your people.
The more they know, the more they'll understand,
and the more they'll care.

Sam Walton, founder, Wal-Mart

As a boy, I was a closet pyromaniac, and I was fascinated with magnifying glasses. Using one of these tools, I could harness random rays of sunlight and channel them through the lens, creating a bead of energy so powerful that I could ignite almost anything.

Now, I can see an amazing correlation between my magnifying glass and the purpose of mission statements and strategic plans. The mission statement and strategic plan are both instruments designed to channel a group's energy toward a common goal. In Chapter One, we discussed the importance of a mission statement and a strategic plan in a leader's quest to realize his or her vision. This chapter shows how communication can bring everyone into the fold, help them share the vision, and "ignite" them to move forward towards the ultimate goal.

With my eyes, I can see it.
With my mind, I can plan it.
With my heart, I must sell it.

Genuine Leader

Communication vs. Information

There is a subtle but profound difference between communication and information. By definition, communication is an exchange of thoughts, ideas, feedback, and/or feelings. It can be two-way, three-way, among a group, or between one person and an audience. Communication can happen anywhere, from coffee shops to online chat rooms to town hall meetings. Communication demands a response.

Information, on the other hand, is a non-interactive dissemination of data, words, stories, or facts. Information is usually conveyed by one entity speaking or writing. Information can be in the form of anything from a memo to a presidential address. Typically, no response is expected.

Information without communication encourages an organization's grapevine and rumor mill to flourish. Associates want to know the "whys" behind pertinent information. Without the opportunity to speak up, talk back, or otherwise interact, workers will tend to complete the incomplete and fill in the blanks on their own. In doing so, they'll commonly rely on a stew of half-truths, rumors, and conjectures. At best, a grapevine is unsettling to an organization's culture; at its worst, it can disrupt the whole workplace environment.

The key to better staff relationships isn't necessarily *more* communication; instead, what's needed is *better* communication. All too often, memos are unilateral directives, conversations are actually shared monologues, meetings become soliloquies, and open-door policies are little more than window dressing.

Genuine Leaders aren't afraid to communicate information in ways that encourage feedback, through meetings, surveys, or suggestion boxes. Genuine Leaders consciously provide information in a communicative setting. Their information is replete with feelings and details that dramatically increase associates' understanding and acceptance of the messages. Pretenders would rather force feed the information to their people through one-way techniques such as telling associates to "take it or leave it."

A strong communication network has the net effect of ensuring greater job security for associates and management. When communication flows in all directions, people form a network that maximizes all the available talents, skills, and personalities. Through communication, we stand united. Through a lack of communication, we fall divided.

Indira Gandhi, the former prime minister of India, said, "I suppose leadership at one time meant muscles, but today it means getting along with people." Genuine Leaders get along with people by building relationships and creating understanding. They are aware of the three skills that they must use in the communication process: **listening, speaking, and writing.** Let's take a closer look at each skill.

LISTENING

There are very few people who don't become more interesting as soon as they stop talking.
Mary Lowry, American author

One of the most precious gifts you can give someone is your undivided attention. Pretenders only look for people who will listen to them. The ability and willingness to listen to peers and team members is the hallmark of a Genuine Leader.

Genuine Leaders know when to stop talking and start

listening. Their adept listening skills allow them to be perceived as caring individuals. Genuine Leaders come across as open-minded and concerned. On the other hand, Pretenders who prefer to dominate conversations come across as pompous and self-centered. In his classic book, *How to Win Friends and Influence People,* Dale Carnegie wrote, "You can make more friends in two months by being interested in other people than you can in two years by trying to have other people be interested in you."

It is the province of knowledge to speak and it is the privilege of wisdom to listen.

Oliver Wendell Holmes, American author and physician

The process of skilled listening has to begin with hearing and seeing everything that's said. You must do more than simply listen to the words. You also have to watch body language, especially facial expressions, and listen intently to the tone of voice. If a subordinate is telling you that everything is going according to plan, but looks and sounds ill at ease, you can be pretty sure that you're not getting the whole story. Ask yourself, "Did I get all the facts? Did I see what he or she really said?"

I once had a mentor who told me that if I listened for the "whispers," I wouldn't have to deal with the "screaming." You should watch for the subtext of what is being said instead of relying only on surface responses.

Former Secretary of State Colin Powell recommends creating a "noisy system," with leadership encouraging an "active and continuing communication of concerns, observations, data, insights, and suggestions from and among employees." In this chapter, we'll describe several techniques that will help you create a "noisy system" in your organization.

When you talk, all you'll know is what you know. But when you listen, you'll know what you know and you'll learn what they know.

Author Unknown

In the movie *Pulp Fiction,* Uma Thurman asks John Travolta a question: "When speaking with someone, do you find yourself intent on listening or waiting for your turn to talk?" This question forced me to examine my own

conversational skills. After some soul-searching, I had to admit that I was probably waiting to talk more often than not. Over time, I've taught myself to give the speaker my full attention instead of planning what to say next.

I'll never forget the lesson that I learned years ago from my oldest daughter, Deanna, who has always had a take-charge attitude. I was working in my home office when Deanna came in to tell me about something special that had happened to her that day in kindergarten. Standing next to my chair, she told her tale with ebullience. I continued to do my work without fully listening. And that's when a five-year-old taught me a lesson that all leaders need to learn.

Recognizing that she didn't have my complete and undivided attention, Deanna reached up to my chin, grabbed a firm hold of my jawbone, and jerked it 90 degrees in her direction. In an instant, I found myself eye-to-eye with a determined little girl. She said, "You weren't listening to me," and proceeded to repeat the entire story face-to-face with my chin in her hand.

I'll always be grateful to her for teaching me how to really listen, not just with my ears but with my eyes, my mind, my heart, and yes, my chin. Today, when I hear the phrase "face time," I know what it means. My daughter Deanna taught me all about it.

Poor Listeners

Poor listeners have some common and noticeable characteristics.
Typically, poor listeners:

- Interrupt the speaker
- Finish the speaker's sentences
- Don't offer visual clues such as nodding or smiling to show that they are listening
- Avoid face/eye contact
- Create physical distractions, such as tapping their pen
- Show impatience by actions like looking at their watch
- Jump to conclusions

I've heard that the average person listens at only 20-25% of his or her potential. What's the explanation for our poor listening habits? Ego, rudeness, lack of time, sleep deprivation, and stress are all common reasons why we don't listen. But these are poor excuses for not paying attention.

I'd like to address one physiological reason why so many of us are such poor listeners. The average human being can only speak at a rate of 100-150

words per minute (wpm), but the average brain can process about 500 wpm. This discrepancy leaves a gap that I call the "Drift Rift." If you talk to me at 150 wpm and my mind is prepared to handle 500 wpm, a rift will result when my mind drifts in search of additional stimuli. While you're talking to me, my mind wants to fill its additional 300+ word capacity, and it begins to wander.

Knowing about the "Drift Rift" has helped me immensely as a presenter. I never stand fixed behind a podium; instead, I move. I always use a variety of audio-visual tools. Without fail, I use a handout with key words left blank, challenging the audience to use more of their cranial capacities. It's my attempt to hold their attention. The next time you hold a conversation or a meeting, be aware of the "Drift Rift" and work harder to occupy more of your listener's attention.

When Leaders Don't Listen

For many bankruptcies and dissolved organizations, there was undoubtedly an employee or middle manager who saw the inevitable demise coming when the leadership didn't. Without a viable communication network for leaders to glean ideas, opinions, and warnings from all levels of the company, a word to the wise may not reach its intended ear.

Worse yet is when the leadership hears the warning but chooses not to act on it because of pride, ego, disbelief, or poor past precedent. Nevertheless, a system needs to be in place so that all the salient information regarding the future health of an organization may reach the leaders.

Imagine if Enron's leadership had paid attention to an August 2001 memo from Sherron Watkins: "I am incredibly nervous that we will implode in a wave of accounting scandals." She sent the memo to her immediate boss, she informed the CEO Kenneth Lay, and she told a friend at the accounting firm of Arthur Andersen. At the time, nobody paid attention to her detailed explanation of what was happening, but the ensuing scandal put Andersen out of business and several members of Enron's management team in jail.

Imagine if people had paid attention to the seven-part series that the New Orleans newspaper *The Times-Picayune* ran in 2002. The series discussed potential hurricane disaster scenarios three years before Katrina crippled the city. The articles detailed several possible situations that actually happened, and included a warning from a professor at Louisiana State University that the levees would fail.

Medical malpractice cases often identify "the failure to listen" as the key problem. At times, the doctor's ego prevents him or her from having a

receptive ear. Other times, the problem may be an inappropriate assumption made after ignoring the patient's remarks and symptoms. The end result from this poor listening could be a deadly misdiagnosis.

The 9/11 Commission determined that the U.S. government had received several specific warnings about hijacked airplanes being flown into buildings long before September 11, 2001. As early as 1995 a captured terrorist gave an explicit threat. Nobody listened.

Of course, you must take the time to find out whether the information is coming from the boy who cried "Wolf!" or from a reliable source who knows more than you do. Every report has to be evaluated. To ignore even the most seemingly bizarre information is to court disaster. Just ask the people at Enron, in New Orleans, in malpractice suits, and in the U.S. government.

Communication Techniques Requiring Only That You Listen

The following six communication techniques are unique – you don't need to speak or write anything. They fall under the category of **The Power of Your Presence.** Never underestimate the power of your presence around the organization. For better or for worse, you have impact on your people without ever opening your mouth or writing a memo.

1. **Think about your body language.** Most leaders are aware that we communicate both verbally and visually. But most leaders don't realize that about 50% of your message is communicated by your body language, especially through your face. As a leader, you must "watch what you say" both literally and figuratively. About 40% of your message is communicated by how you sound – your tone, pitch, volume, and inflection. Only about 10% of your message is communicated by the words that you actually say.

For example, if I say to you, "I like your hat," you might be glad that you bought it. However, if I wrinkle my nose, squint my eyes, and use a condescending tone, you might interpret my comment entirely differently. By using a negative tone of voice and negative body motions, you can send a very negative message even when you use absolutely positive words.

2. **Practice "Management by Walking Around."** Just being visible and showing your interest in the day-to-day operations can act as positive communication. Indeed, the presence of a Genuine Leader in the workplace is a plus. But be warned: this technique must be used in moderation. You want to project enthusiasm and approachability. The last thing that your team needs is an army drill sergeant who micromanages every detail of the operation.

3. **Initiate a "Work-as-a-Clerk" program.** This is a program that I created to keep my leadership close to the day-to-day operations. For four-hour intervals each month, my management and I donned the appropriate uniform to work as clerks in different areas of the organization. Listening and observing gave me valuable information about what was really going on in my company.

David Neeleman, the founder of JetBlue Airways, used the "work-as-a-clerk" technique. He personally served passengers on the planes, introducing himself and asking people to give their opinions of his airline. He regularly showed up as a baggage handler or at the ticket desk. The associates appreciated his face-to-face approach to the issues they dealt with every day. The customers also appreciated the extra effort. Even after weather issues in February 2007 kept several loaded planes on the runway for hours on end, JetBlue flights remain booked to capacity. Neeleman's customers have remained fiercely loyal to a company that obviously cares deeply about them.

4. **Eat lunch in the associate's break room.** Don't sit in a corner with fellow executives; instead, join a group of lower-level associates and listen to their professional as well as personal issues.

5. **Ask permission to attend a manager's meeting.** Be a fly on the wall – listen, don't talk. See first-hand how your managers handle themselves with their teams. Conscientious school principals do the same thing when they periodically audit specific classes.

6. **Sit in and observe a key associate's performance review.** You may want to do this with an associate who has shown great promise or who holds a vital position in the company. By listening to the exchange between the associate and his or her supervisors, you will learn a lot more about everyone involved in the review. We'll discuss the review process in greater detail in Chapter Seven.

SPEAKING

The most valuable of all talents is that of never using two words when one will do.

Thomas Jefferson, American president

There are five basic "Speaking" scenarios:

- Conversing one-on-one
- Addressing a group
- Conducting a meeting
- Giving a directive
- Asking a question

Let's take a brief look at each.

The One-on-One Conversation

Have you ever been in a conversation with someone who constantly looks over your shoulder as if seeking someone more important to talk to? The one-to-one interchange is only successful when each person pays complete attention to what's being said. Look the other person in the eye. Stay close without invading his or her personal space. Respect the other person's right to express a thought without interruption. If you're discussing an important matter, give a quick summary of what you both decided before ending the conversation.

Addressing a Group

I was 23 years old when I made my first major business presentation to an audience of 600 people. I couldn't eat or sleep for the two days preceding the event. When it was over, I thought my performance was awful. But I did it. Each and every subsequent presentation has been easier and more fun. Today, I'm still a little nervous before a presentation, but what I feel most is excitement mixed with the hope that my audience and I will connect in a meaningful way.

A couple of years later, I was planning our annual Associate Awards meeting. For a guest speaker, I wanted Frank Perdue, the best-known man in the chicken business and an icon in the supermarket industry. At the time, Mr. Perdue was on TV all the time, in humorous commercials for his company. I figured my associates would get a real kick out of seeing him in person. His reply to my invitation to speak at our meeting was this brief, handwritten note from the legend himself:

September 8, 1982

Dear Harold,

Thanks for your invitation for Jan. '83, but a public speaker I am not. It is truly a chore I never relish, though I necessarily must address our own employees and customers periodically.

It is an honor, however, and perhaps I can do something else of not such an embarrassing nature sometime.

Frank Perdue

Since I had never met Mr. Perdue before, I was truly impressed by the personal note and how he candidly shared his fear of public speaking.

But my advice to you: don't avoid speaking opportunities like Frank Perdue did. Never give up trying to become a more accomplished speaker. Public speaking is the number one fear for most people, ranking higher than divorce, heights, or death. But even the most extreme stage fright can be overcome. Join a Toastmasters International chapter (www.toastmasters.org) in your area where you can practice speaking in front of a friendly audience. A few books that will help you learn more about public speaking are listed at the end of this chapter. One thing that every book and performance coach agrees on is that you must practice constantly if you want to feel comfortable speaking to an audience. The second thing that all the experts agree on is, as Lee Iacocca suggests, "talking to people in their own language." You want your audience to say, "Wow, he/she said exactly what I was thinking."

Five Rules to Remember when Making a Presentation:

Rule 1. Be yourself and let your passion shine through your words. Your listeners want to know what makes you tick, what pushes your buttons, what makes you jump up and down with enthusiasm. Being passionate beats being mechanical every time.

Rule 2. Study, understand, and respect your audience, whether they number 1 or 1,000. Their faces will mirror your speaking ability. President Lyndon Johnson once said, "You ain't learning nothin' when you're talking." I must respectfully disagree. When giving a presentation, I watch my audiences intently while I'm speaking and they teach me a great deal. Their expressions tell me instantly when I need to adjust my tone, movement, speed of delivery, or subject matter to get them back on track with me.

I do not object to people looking at
their watches when I am speaking.
But I strongly object when they start shaking them
to make certain they are still going.

Lord Birkett, British barrister and judge

Rule 3. Never speak about anything you're not interested in. This rule sounds simplistic, but many professional speakers will sometimes accept any booking for the experience or the speaking fee. Never be coerced into talking about something you can't be passionate about. Your audience will immediately spot you as an imposter.

After eating an entire bull,
a mountain lion felt so good he started to roar.
He kept roaring until
a hunter came along and shot him.
The moral: When you're full of bull,
keep your mouth shut.

Will Rogers, American humorist

Rule 4. Be concise. A great tip for speakers is to stop talking before you run out of meaningful things to say. This means that you'll have to take more time to prepare what you're going to say. Rambling is easy. Being concise takes work, but it's worth it.

Rule 5. Allow for silence in your talk or conversation. Silence allows your audience's thoughts to catch up, lets them complete their notes, and allows them to form questions. If you strategically inject brief moments of silence into your presentation, you'll be able to study the audience's reaction and diagnose the impact that you are – or are not – having on them.

Silences regulate the flow of listening and talking.
They are to conversations what zeroes
are to mathematics – crucial nothings without
which communication can't work.

Gerald Goodman, communications expert

Speaking effectively in public was once merely considered to be a plus for the up-and-coming executive. Now, public speaking has become a requirement for leaders on every level. Your ability to speak drives your ability to influence, and your ability to influence will drive your ability to successfully lead people.

Conducting a Meeting

At their best, meetings can build businesses and profits. But, at their worst, meetings can waste money and kill projects. A well-run meeting always depends on preparation.

Here are a dozen techniques that you can use to run a successful meeting:

1. **Prepare.** Plan to spend at least as much time preparing for a meeting as you will take to conduct it. What are the objectives? What issues will appear on the agenda? In what order should they be presented? Usually, you'll want to limit your agenda to no more than eight topics. If the agenda is too long, you won't be able to address all the issues, and you'll lose the attendees' attention.

2. **Provide an outline ahead of time.** When possible and appropriate, give attendees an outline of the meeting's objectives a day or two in advance. With some lead time, they will be able to prepare their thoughts and gather information to be ready for the meeting.

3. **Limit attendance.** Try to keep the attendance for most meetings between 5 and 15 people. Fewer than 5 limits the amount of input and can make the meeting feel too informal. More than 15 attendees make the gathering unwieldy. If you can't read the facial expression of every participant within seconds of a poignant remark, you probably have too many people in attendance.

4. **Plan the seating arrangement.** Shy people and newcomers tend to slip into the background. Whether you use a circular, rectangular, or horseshoe-shaped seating arrangement, all participants must be kept in the loop, both physically and psychologically. A welcoming seating arrangement encourages a feeling of belonging and increases participation.

5. **Greet the participants.** Say hello to the participants when they arrive, just as you would greet guests visiting your home. Offer a copy of the final agenda as they enter. Make sure that beverages, notepaper, and pens are available.

6. **Review the ground rules.** Before beginning the meeting, always reiterate the ground rules for the proceedings. I suggest these two rules: One, all participants should restrict each response to two minutes or less, to keep the meeting moving efficiently. Two, personal issues should be reserved for a one-to-one discussion at another time. Group meetings aren't the right venue to

hear about someone's isolated problem with his or her paycheck.

7. **Select an "official" note-taker/reporter.** At the start of the meeting, let everyone know that you'll be choosing someone to report on the main resolutions reached during the meeting. By doing it this way, everyone will pay more attention and take more detailed notes because they may be chosen to do the summary at the end. A fun icebreaker is to select the reporter by spinning a bottle.

8. **Maximize participation.** Discussion of each issue should begin with a volunteer and proceed in either a clockwise or counterclockwise fashion around the group. Using this orderly procedure, no one can be left out. Those who don't wish to comment at a particular time can simply state, "I'll pass." Make sure that those passing do make a contribution the next time around.

The group leader can increase participation by asking that everyone write down responses to a particular question or idea before speaking. That way, the more reserved individuals in the group can simply read their responses rather than speaking extemporaneously. The leader's primary objective should be to maximize participation and minimize embarrassment.

9. **Maximize attention.** Always begin with the issue that involves the most people in the room. This ensures maximum interest from the participants. The last issue on the agenda should preferably be upbeat and positive, such as, "What one thing did you do since our last meeting that went really well and helped us move toward achieving our objective?"

10. **Limit the meeting length.** Ideally, a meeting should last between 45 and 75 minutes. Meetings should rarely last more than 90 minutes. Longer meetings are less effective because attention wanders, attendees want to get back to work, and there are probably so many issues on the table that nothing seems very important.

11. **Summarize meeting results.** The final 10 minutes of a meeting should be reserved for summarizing the final decisions made on each of the issues discussed. Ask the official note-taker to read the resolutions, emphasizing, "Who is going to do what by when?" All participants will leave the meeting with a clearer understanding of the next steps that they need to take.

12. **Communicate results.** When appropriate, use your department bulletin board to communicate the results of your meeting to the associates who didn't attend. Throughout the month between meetings, you should cross off those issues that have been successfully addressed. Soon, associates will be more interested in participating in your meetings because they'll see that you listen, commit, take action, and follow through.

Giving A Directive

Leaders need to give direction all the time. Pretenders will dictate orders. A Genuine Leader says "please" and "thank you" when giving a directive. It's appalling how many people in leadership positions fail to give their associates this common courtesy. If leaders took the time to read the facial expressions of the people they're directing, they would see how poorly abrupt commands are received. No one likes to be barked at. Associates shouldn't be treated like plebes at West Point.

Be aware of Parkinson's Law: "Work expands so as to fill the time available for its completion." In 1958, C. Northcote Parkinson promulgated this theory in *Parkinson's Law: The Pursuit of Progress*, a commentary on the inefficiencies of British government and business. He observed that the government and private companies tended to hire too many staffers for the amount of work available. This meant that more people had more time to accomplish less.

Parkinson was right on target. When there are firm deadlines, amazing amounts of additional work can be done in short periods of time without hiring additional people. Conversely, without time constraints, people feel no reason to hurry, so tasks take longer.

Duke Ellington once said, "I don't need time. I need a deadline." Make Parkinson's Law work in your favor. When you give your associates a directive, assign a deadline for the task.

I once asked a new associate to sweep up the parking area and restaurant entrance. When I noticed that he hadn't returned an hour later, I went to check on him. No, he wasn't goofing off. Instead, he was doing a far better job than I needed or wanted. I was reminded to use Parkinson's Law to my advantage. I should have said, "Please take 30 minutes and a broom to sweep up around the building and parking lot." A Genuine Leader recognizes that time parameters add needed structure to any directive.

Asking a Question

A good question is a work of art that catalyzes the conversation. If you ask a poor question, you'll receive a useless response – G.I.G.O. (Garbage In, Garbage Out).

I was lucky enough to learn the art of question crafting from Dr. Michael Kolivosky, the dean of the Dow Leadership Center at Hillsdale College in Michigan. He taught me the value of a good "prober question" in obtaining information that you can use. A prober question invites participation and

stimulates thinking. It moves from the general to the specific and points the conversation in a purposeful direction.

Here's how Dr. Kolivosky describes the characteristics of a good prober question:

a. **It's Personal.** Dr. Kolivosky suggests that pronouns such as *you, your,* and *we* be included in the question. For example, begin your query with, "In your opinion…" or "How could we…?" or "Do you think…?"

b. **It's Constructive.** The question should be phrased positively. Don't ask for a laundry list of complaints. Instead, inquire, "What one improvement do you think could be made?"

c. **It's Specific to a Single Topic.** Dr. Kolivosky warns against a double-barreled question because it divides the focus. Don't ask, "What is the best way for us to build sales and reduce costs?" Instead, ask two separate questions.

d. **It's Selective.** The professor points to words such as *one, single, best,* and *most* as good ways elicit a person's top priority response. For example, "What is the single best idea you have to…?"

e. **It's Involving.** Dr. Kolivosky advises that a question should seek action on the part of the other person or people. This action may take the form of involvement or commitment rather than a mere exchange of words. For example, "What would be the one most effective way that you could improve the sales of our products?"

f. **It's Concise.** A good question should be clear and brief. A clear, concise query generally yields a clear, concise answer. For example, "In your opinion, is this the best course of action for us to take?"

Questioning can either be Garbage In, Garbage Out – or Substance In, Substance Out. It's your choice.

WRITING

Everything official, sooner or later,
gets written down.
And what you say is what you get.
It has to be clear, concise, and correct.

Dianna Booher, motivational speaker and author

If you've been fortunate enough to receive a handwritten note of thanks or congratulations from an authority figure whose opinion you value, you remember the positive impact that it made on you. If you're like others I've spoken with, you've saved the note. Handwritten notes are especially powerful in today's electronic world. Typed messages and faxes work fine, but nothing is more prized than the handwritten note of gratitude or praise.

So why don't more leaders write notes and letters by hand? Some leaders are embarrassed to show their poor penmanship, bad grammar, lack of vocabulary, misspellings, or disorganization on paper. Others think that giving a written commendation could trigger a request for a raise, or could come back to haunt them later if the relationship sours. And everyone claims they don't have enough time to write handwritten notes.

Pretenders will use any excuse to avoid putting their thoughts into writing. But Genuine Leaders know that the amount of time and effort it takes to hand write a note is worth it because of the huge morale boost that it provides. Don't fall back on excuses – get writing!

Here are seven tried-and-true ways that leaders use the written word to improve productivity, enhance communications, and reward associates.

1. **Send letters.** An annual letter that you send to all your associates at their homes lets you communicate with your associates and their families. Topics might include the current state of the company, a new benefit announcement, or an issue that has hit or will soon hit the media.

2. **Create a functional bulletin board that is divided into three sections.** Use the first section for federal regulations (e.g., minimum wage posters, etc.). The second section is for company policies, announcements, time schedules, and for newsworthy notes. Reserve the final area for topics pertinent to events of yesterday, today, or tomorrow. This third section of the board will be changed and read most often, and it will reduce team

members' dependency on a rumor-based grapevine. Be certain to update all the bulletin board information on a regular basis.

3. **Use a written assignment sheet / to-do list.** This clear written document can be an excellent communication device if used properly. At the end of this chapter, you'll see a sample assignment sheet that can be adapted for use in a variety of organizations.

4. **Take attitude surveys.** These should be conducted on an annual basis and will provide you with a rich database of associate insight. People always want to tell you what they think and how they feel when they perceive you as caring.

5. **Install a suggestion box.** The old reliable suggestion box, updated each month with a new message or question, really does work. It's important that your associates understand that there will be no negative consequences for freely expressing their opinions. Post suggestions that really make a difference on the bulletin board. Associates need to see that you listen and react to their legitimate comments and requests.

6. **Enclose information in the paycheck envelope.** This information can be a formal announcement important to everyone in the company or an informal, handwritten note with a message for one specific person.

7. **Use "You Did Great!" stationery.** You can use this type of handwritten note to recognize associates who go above and beyond expectations. Aim to mail out one "You Did Great!" note per every 20 associates under your leadership each month. The rewards will be huge.

I heard what you said, but talk is cheap... Put it in writing and impress me.

Genuine Leader

SUMMARY SCORE:

It's time to quantify your ability to communicate on a 1-10 scale. You could receive up to 5 (of the 10) points for being a superb listener. Up to 3 points for being a great speaker. And 2 points for being a skilled writer. The leader who is a superior listener, speaker, and writer would receive a total top score of 10.

How do you measure up?

Recommendations to Raise Your *Listening* Score:

1. Remind yourself that listening is a very active process and that it's the necessary precursor to all great decisions and actions.

Focus on the speaker's eyes when listening intently. Use a notepad to store your thoughts so as not to interrupt. At the end, review what you believe to be the next step with the speaker.

2. **Institute Colin Powell's "noisy system" in your organization.**

If your people perceive you as caring and a sincere listener, they will talk to you. If everyone participates in the flow of communication, you'll have a well-functioning network.

3. **Never forget all the components of communication: 50% body language, 40% tone of voice, and 10% the words you use.**

Remember that about 90% of your communicated message is essentially non-verbal.

4. **Listen before speaking.**

The next time that you find yourself ready to jump to a conclusion or interrupt someone talking to you, stop! Begin to listen more intently. You'll be more enjoyable to converse with, and you'll be amazed at what you'll learn.

Recommendations to Raise Your *Speaking* Score:

1. **Be the first.**

When it comes to speaking with one or more people, always be the first to greet the others. "Breaking the ice" allows for openness and dialogue. Forget posturing and timidity. Instead, extend your hand and say, "Hello, I'm ..."

2. **Criticize only in private.**

Although we all know this, we see people break this rule all too often. Few things will destroy your ability to lead others faster than embarrassing your staff by criticizing them in public.

3. **Practice, practice, practice.**

Cut your teeth as a speaker in places where the expectations may not be so high. For example, volunteer to speak at fundraisers or at your local high school's career day. Offer to make a toast to a departing colleague. These lower-pressure environments will make you more comfortable with performing in public. You may still be nervous, but you will be getting the essential practice in small steps.

4. **Get feedback.**

After a speech, ask a random selection of people from your audience to assess your presentation using a pre-printed, simple evaluation form. Invite

them to comment on your preparation, your presentation's content, your delivery, and the subject's relevance. Their feedback will help you improve your skills for your next speaking opportunity.

5. **Have an open door policy.**

The standard open door policy invites associates to discuss issues of importance one-on-one with their leader. It's a good idea to set aside scheduled times each week when you'll be readily available.

6. **Utilize daily "huddle-ups."**

In these 10-minute meetings, up to 15 representatives from around the organization gather at the beginning of a shift to share information about the hours ahead.

7. **Hold regular department meetings.**

These longer meetings should be scheduled weekly or monthly, and they should focus on issues related to each specific department.

8. **Consider a "Good Morning" announcement.**

Where an intercom exists, leaders and associates can communicate to everyone simultaneously at the beginning of the day.

9. **Consider T.E.A.M. meetings.**

T.E.A.M. is an acronym for Thoughts Exchanged by Associates and Management. This type of meeting is one of the most effective communication techniques I've ever used. Associates from each area within the organization meet to discuss concerns or issues of interest without the presence of their immediate managers. The meetings occur monthly and last 90 minutes.

I got the idea from President Franklin D. Roosevelt's famous fireside chats, adapting them into conversations instead of monologues.

Recommendations to Raise Your *Writing* Score:

1. **Handwrite one letter of thanks each month and mail it to a special performer in your organization.**

Also, write one personal note of gratitude per week. Use a Post-it® note and stick it on your associate's windshield, desk, or computer screen. These notes will hone your writing skills, boost your team's morale, and will make people proud to follow you.

2. **Handwritten wins hands down.**

Teach your managers that it's okay to use email and faxes to inform their people, but a handwritten memo is always a much more effective communication tool.

3. **Create a sloppy copy first.**

When writing an important letter or report, use the drafting technique that you learned in middle school. First, jot down your most salient thoughts on the subject. Then create a "sloppy copy," stringing together your ideas into roughly written sentences and paragraphs. Next, re-write your sloppy copy in semi-final form and give it to two trusted advisors for review. Finally, incorporate their constructive comments into your final draft. Your completed letter or presentation will be something you will be proud of.

4. **Use written assignment sheets or to-do lists daily.**

Here's a sample.

ASSOCIATE ASSIGNMENT SHEET			
Department: _____		Date:_____	
Assigned To	Description of Work	E.T.C. in Minutes	Check when Completed
	1.		
	2.		
	3.		
	4.		
	5.		
	6.		
	7.		
	8.		
	9.		
	10.		

Rules for Using an Associate Assignment Sheet:
1. List only variable work activities, not routine and obvious fixed activities.
2. Use *Estimated Time to Complete* Column (E.T.C). Remember Parkinson's Law?
3. Total *Estimated Time to Complete* column must not exceed 30 minutes of work per four-hour shift. They have their fixed activities to perform.
4. Employees should experience the satisfaction of completing 3 of 5 assignment sheets.
5. Use "fresh-made" Assignment Sheets.

RECOMMENDED READING
➥ "I Can See You Naked," A Fearless Guide to Making Great Presentations
by Ron Hoff *(Andrews McMeel, 1988)*
➥ The Seven Strategies of Master Presenters
by Brad McRae and David Brooks *(Career Press, 2004)*
➥ Listening: The Forgotten Skill: A Self-Teaching Guide
by Madelyn Burley-Allen *(Wiley, 1995)*
➥ The 7 Powers of Questions: Secrets to Successful Communication in Life and at Work
by Dorothy Leeds *(Perigee Trade, 2000)*
➥ Gremlins of Grammar: A Guide to Conquering the Mischievous Myths that Plague American English
by Toni Boyle and K. D. Sullivan *(McGraw-Hill, 2006)*

GENUINE LEADERS
KNOW THE NUMBERS

It has been my experience that competency
in mathematics enhances a person's ability
to handle the more ambiguous and qualitative
relationships that dominate our
day-to-day decision-making.

Alan Greenspan, American economist

Any organizational endeavor's success is best measured with numbers. Although a leader doesn't have to know how to perform every function within his/her span of control, he or she must be able to read and understand the performance indicators of each of those functions. A leader must also be able to detect impending problems and spot wide-open opportunities before they slip away to the competition.

Genuine Leaders are capable of making decisive and calculated decisions based on facts and figures rather than on feelings and emotions.

For example, a decision to sell a company's original headquarters office building might be emotionally charged. A Pretender will give a lot of consideration to the aggravation involved in the move and would focus on the conflicts and difficulties of the decision. A Genuine Leader who knows the costs associated with maintaining an older building and the benefits of moving to a new location will be able to see that the decision to sell is straightforward. The emotional ties can be cut with less pain when you recognize that the result is a $32,000-per-year rent savings, an $87,000 reduction in HVAC costs, and a 17% drop in transportation expense.

Numbers add color and clarity

Even the most math-phobic among us uses numbers everyday to make a point, stimulate interest, or influence a decision. For instance:

• If I told you, "Desert sands get hot during the day," you might yawn and respond, "Yeah, so what?" But if I told you, "The desert sands can get as hot as 176°F, while water boils between 186-212°F," these numbers would provide you a frame of reference, and you might be a bit more interested.

• If I told you that a lot of baseballs are used during a major league baseball game, you might respond, "No kidding." But if I told you that the average life of a baseball is nine pitches, that piece of trivia might cause you to listen up.

• If the doctor told you that your blood pressure was high, you might admit you need to eat better and exercise more. But if the doctor said that your blood pressure was 180/110, 30% worse than at your last checkup, you might take more immediate action to improve.

• If we were co-managers and I told you that our sales were up last week over the same week last year, you might say, "Good." But if I told you that our sales were up 8.1 percent and that we were leading all divisions, you might be a whole lot more enthusiastic, especially if our bonuses were tied to that number.

The judicious use of specific numbers "fills in the blanks." Numbers help us paint the picture and complete the incomplete. Using numbers to integrate goals and directives provides greater clarity for your team and is much more likely to stimulate a positive reaction.

To fully utilize the power of numbers, Genuine Leaders:

1. Know the important critical numbers and how they have been generated.
2. Manage the numbers to the benefit of the organizations.
3. Share the numbers with others who need to know them.
4. Motivate others with numerical goals.

Let's take a closer look at each of these requirements.

1. Genuine Leaders KNOW the Numbers

There are probably several thousand ways to use numbers to evaluate an organization's performance. Commonly used performance standards that involve numbers are Return On Investment, Earnings Before Interest and Taxes, and Sales per Hour. Other performance standards could include Tons per Day, Visits per Week, Complaints per 1000, and many more.

Genuine Leaders know the critical numbers that accurately measure their organization's performance. By focusing on a few critical indicators, they can use the numbers masterfully to diagnose the health of their organization.

Food service operators can often be particularly skilled at knowing the numbers. In an effort to locate the source of a lower than acceptable food cost percentage, I solicited the help of our franchise advisor. He had 15 years experience with the company and was thoroughly numbers-savvy. When I told him about our unexplained 1.7% food cost shortfall, he immediately said, "If you're missing more than 1.5% of your food cost for two consecutive periods, you have at least one voracious thief working for you."

Although I was skeptical of his quick diagnosis – I thought, "None of my employees would steal from me!" – I was impressed by his emphatic statement. A few weeks later, we discovered that one of our newly promoted assistant managers had managed to embezzle several thousand dollars over a period of six months. If I hadn't learned our advisor's "rule of thumb" regarding these numbers, I would never have focused on looking for an internal thief and wouldn't have solved our chronic problem. As we discussed in Chapter Two, I had to "find the tick" to identify what the real problem was before we could solve it.

During a televised Denver Broncos vs. Baltimore Ravens football game one night, the announcers were discussing what the Broncos' coach, Mike Shanahan, considers to be the most important number in determining the teams that will ultimately play in the Super Bowl. Coach Shanahan had figured out that the team with the best "take-away vs. turnover ratio" (fumbles lost vs. recovered and interceptions made vs. lost) had historically done well in the playoffs. In fact, the announcers said that 10 out of the top 11 teams in the league with respect to this ratio had made it into the playoffs the year before.

Coach Shanahan is, no doubt, a talented coach. He recognized that this one relatively obscure ratio seemed to hold the key to success in the NFL. Coach Shanahan uses this ratio to measure his team's performance and to guide their weekly practices. Turnover training has become a big part of the Broncos pre-game preparation. They believe that managing this ratio gives them a strategic advantage.

The next day, after the Broncos had won, I read in the paper that the Broncos had had a +2 advantage in the takeaway/turnover ratio for that game against the Ravens. Coach Shanahan apparently knows his numbers.

2. Genuine Leaders MANAGE the Numbers

"If you can't measure it, you won't be able to manage it." Many authors, including management guru Peter Drucker, are given credit for first saying this phrase. I believe that truer words were never spoken. I'll forever be grateful to the person who first taught me this saying. It has to be one of the top ten best bits of advice I've ever received.

This phrase may be applied to almost any situation. Consider a weight management program. Without a scale and a unit of measurement, you'll never be able to keep track of your desired weight. Jump on the scale, and you can track your progress immediately.

How about improving employee relations? Depending on whether you listen to your Squeaky Wheels or your Apple Polishers, you could get conflicting viewpoints about this issue. But read the employee turnover report or the employee attitude survey results regularly, and you'll be able to pinpoint problems and manage your employee relations a whole lot better than you could based solely on subjective opinions.

Genuine Leaders know that every endeavor must be accompanied by a method to measure its progress. Whether handing out an assignment or receiving a task yourself, it's vital to make sure that all parties involved are aware of the performance standards and how they will be measured. This rule holds true whether the numbers involve…

- Payroll %
- Earned run average
- Miles per gallon
- Minutes per mile
- Cases per day
- Inventory turns
- Price accuracy %

- People per shift
- Rings per minute
- New products per year
- On-time arrival %
- Overtime hours used
- Days lost
- Service level %

Most processes can be measured in a specific, numeric fashion. Genuine Leaders won't rest until the process has at least one measurement mechanism designed to assess its progress. Otherwise, they know that they'll never be able to manage it.

Being able to fix an anomaly or adjust an aberration are important skills when managing the numbers. Knowing the cause-and-effect relationship between relevant numbers can mean the difference between a quick, accurate solution and a pesky problem that becomes chronic.

In a meeting with all the company's department heads, I asked one manager why his gross margin was 2% lower than that of the previous quarter. His response was instantaneous and illuminating. He said, "Because our advertising was not as "hot" (low-priced) as it was last quarter."

The fact that his answer wasn't a joke and the lack of laughter from his peers unnerved me. What he said, and what the others were admitting to without knowing it, was that none of them knew the causal relationship between pricing and gross margins.

After administering a formal numbers exercise to all my managers, I discovered that I had a lot of work to do. Over 60 percent of the managers couldn't pass my 20-question quiz about the pertinent numbers of our business. If my managers lacked an intimate understanding of how our critical numbers were generated and what impacted them, I'd never be able to maximize our organization's profitability. I immediately set out on a mission to educate everyone on what the critical numbers were and how to manage them.

Control your expenses
        better than your competition.
This is where you can always find
                a competitive advantage.

Sam Walton, founder, Wal-Mart

Southwest knows its numbers

In its infancy, the owners of Southwest Airlines looked at their industry's numbers analytically and determined that they didn't have a snowball's chance in hell of running their airline the traditional way if they wanted their business to take off. The founders decided to create their own model, which eventually revolutionized the airline industry.

Rollin King, John Parker, and Herb Kelleher wanted to create a low-cost, no-frills airline that provided the best service at the lowest rates. To accomplish this goal, they needed to be the most efficient and lowest cost operator in the business. These three leaders completely changed the business model for airlines by changing key numbers, which resulted in huge savings and profitability. They standardized their fleet by using only the Boeing 737, which reduced maintenance and training costs. They acquired gates at less congested, secondary airports, where the landing fees were much lower. And they studied ultra-efficient Indy car racing pits to learn how to "turn" their planes in just 15 minutes, 75% faster than the industry average.

When I contacted Southwest's president, Colleen Barrett, to ask if their strategic plan had changed during their more than two decades of operation, her proud response was, "Our commitment to being the lowest-cost, lowest-priced operator has enabled us to achieve 21 consecutive years of profitable growth." The Genuine Leaders at Southwest know and manage the numbers.

3. Genuine Leaders SHARE the Numbers

Leaders who keep their numbers
"close to their vest"
end up losing their shirt.

Genuine Leader

In employee meetings, I've always enjoyed asking new staff members to try to guess the profit margin percentage in supermarket retailing. This is one

of the first steps that they have to take to better understand the "penny profit" challenge the supermarket business faces each and every day.

At first, new associates are incredulous when I tell them that a customer purchasing $100 worth of groceries actually contributes, after taxes, about $1 to our bottom line. This figure opens their eyes to the importance of watching our expenses and containing costs. With this understanding, they feel more empowered and better able to participate in the objective of achieving above-average profitability.

Justify it with numbers

When times were tough and money was tight, I always felt bad telling a manager that his or her pet project had to be put on the back burner. The look of disappointment on the face of one of my stars was hard for me to take, because I knew that he or she wanted the funds to make our company better, not just for his or her own personal benefit.

When times were good and money was available, I still found myself in a similar quandary when trying to decide which pet project we should invest in. Some of my people couldn't understand why their project wasn't being funded. To solve this dilemma, I created the Project to Improve Performance report (a P.I.P. example is at the end of this chapter).

The report was designed to show my managers how to calculate a simple Return on Investment (R.O.I.), using numbers to justify a major capital expenditure. It allowed me to prioritize the projects based on their profitability, not on emotional opinions. Of course, some projects achieved top priority status because of external reasons such as a government mandate or a safety issue; the rest were prioritized by their R.O.I. values.

It became far easier for me to explain – and far easier for my managers to accept – a simple R.O.I. analysis that showed them how all of the ideas on the table were prioritized objectively.

7 X 7 Critical Matrix

One day, my vice president of finance deposited a ream of computer printouts on my desk. He told me that it was the quarterly financial report. After thumbing through the enormous piles, I knew that I had to do something drastic and immediate to make these numbers more manageable. First of all, there wasn't enough time in the day for me to invest in gleaning the salient information from that heap of paper. And how was I going to share the pertinent facts from the mess on my desk with the rest of my associates? They had neither the time nor the expertise to wade through it all. Remembering how helpful Cliff's Notes® summaries had been for me as a student, I decided to create a Cliff's Notes version of the enormous quarterly financial report.

Soon, my vice-president of finance, my operations director, and I created our "7 x 7 Critical Matrix." We determined the seven key numbers that indicated the direction our company was going and degree of success we were having. Next, we divided a timeline into seven periods (weeks, months, quarters, etc.) so that we could fully delineate the direction we were taking. The seven key numbers plotted over the seven periods of time resulted in our 7 x 7 Critical Matrix. In effect, we condensed a tower of data down to one 8-1/2 x 11 sheet of paper.

Here is a sample 7 x 7 Critical Matrix:

7 x 7 CRITICAL MATRIX REPORT

Period (Monthly, Quarterly, etc)	1	2	3	4	5	6	7
1. Sales (+ or -) (Weekly)	+3.1%	+1.3%	+2.7%	-4.1%	+3.2%	+6.1%	+3.9%
2. Payroll % Sales (Weekly)	9.6%	9.4%	9.4%	9.7%	10.1%	9.5%	9.4%
3. Customer Count (+or-)	+608	+128	+173	+210	+317	+154	+213
4. Avg. Sale per Customer (Weekly)	31.21	29.88	30.73	30.12	31.62	32.71	34.06
5. Employee Turnover % (Quarterly)	19%	30%	16%	24%	7%	18%	21%
6. Total Membership (+or-)	+76	+12	+43	+7	+12	+21	+17
7. Adv. as a % of Sales (Monthly)	2.1%	2.7%	2.9%	2.8%	2.8%	3.1%	3.0%

The 7 x 7 Critical Matrix Report is a numerical summary of the health of an organization. This one-page document is both a vital report card and road map. It helped my managers spot trends much sooner than before. The numbers and ratios that you choose to follow will depend on your specific type of business/organization as well as what you and your peers decide will most accurately portray your organization's financial standing.

Genuine Leaders MOTIVATE/ CHALLENGE their associates with numbers

Numbers provide tangible, objective, universally understood targets that guide your associates' efforts to achieve their objectives.

Pretenders ask for "improved sales." Genuine Leaders ask for a 4.7% increase in sales. Pretenders demand "payroll cuts." Genuine Leaders target a specific number.

There's an old story about the senior Charles Schwab when he was the president of U. S. Steel in the early 1900s. While visiting an underperforming steel mill one day, Schwab asked the mill manager how many "heats," or smelting cycles, they had run that day. The manager responded that his shift had made six heats. Schwab then took a piece of chalk and wrote a big *6* on the floor in full view of all employees.

When the second shift arrived that afternoon, many of the workers asked what the *6* on the floor signified. The word got around that the first shift had made six heats that day. The story goes that by the next morning, the *6* on the floor had been erased and a bigger number *7* had been written in its place.

I'm not sure exactly how long it took, but when Charles Schwab visited that plant again, he saw a huge *10* on the floor exactly where he had earlier written the original *6*. The poorest performing steel mill in the company had risen to become the number one producer. When asked how he had accomplished this feat, Charles Schwab said, "The way to get things done is to stimulate competition." To make that principle work for you, you need to know the numbers.

The Charles Schwab anecdote is just one of hundreds of stories about how numbers can be used to motivate people. In the world of long-distance running, spotters at each mile marker continuously call out the time elapsed during the race – "8 minutes, 6 seconds; 12 minutes, 9 seconds," etc. This information tells the runners where they are time-wise, and how fast they need to go to achieve their goals. Genuine Leaders use numbers to let their people know where they are and how much more they have to do to achieve their goals.

I was invited to attend a client's annual sales meeting in which the president announced that the company's sales goal for the year was a 7.1% increase. Instantly, the facial reactions of those in the room reflected surprise and skepticism. Apparently, at no time in recent memory had the company achieved such a large sales increase. However, the autocratic president was oblivious to the facial messages that his managers were sending. Instead, he moved on to the next topic on the agenda.

During a break, I asked the president if he had noticed the looks of doubt on the managers' faces. I suggested that he restate the sales goal a bit differently. Instead of a blanket 7.1% sales increase, I recommended a by-store, by-department, by-day, and by-the-hour sales goal. If each department in each store generated $18 more sales per hour each day, seven days a week, this company could achieve an overall sales bump of over eight percent.

When the break was over, the president restated his goal on a sales-per-department-per-hour basis instead of the overall 7.1% increase. After some discussion, not a manager in the room seemed to doubt that the company could increase sales by $18 per hour in all departments. The mood of the meeting lightened. The challenge before them now seemed doable. An incomprehensible sales goal became feasible when it was broken down into

bite-size pieces. Although they missed their mark by .4%, the team succeeded in achieving the highest sales increase that the company had seen in over seven years.

Numbers can be used to motivate customers as well as employees. Harrah's Entertainment, Inc. wanted to identify its best customers and reward them in new ways. The leaders instituted a "Total Rewards" loyalty program to identify the "low-rollers," a profitable segment that had been previously ignored and undervalued. They determined that these small gamblers, who spent no more than $50 per visit, represented 40% of Harrah's business.

Once Harrah's realized that they were under-serving these customers, they redesigned the casino floors to include a higher percentage of lower-denomination slot machines and video poker games. The new design resulted in a 12% hike in slot revenues and an overall 12% increase in earnings. Genuine Leaders know how to motivate everyone with numbers.

Another leader who understands how to motivate by numbers is Jack Stack, president and CEO of Springfield Remanufacturing Corporation (SRC). In his book, *The Great Game of Business,* Stack tells how, as a young manager, he succeeded in turning around a factory that International Harvester had told him to sell or shut down. Stack is a pioneer in the school of Open Book Management. He teaches every member of his team how to be a business person, shares information with them, and thus enables them to act for the good of the company.

Stack says, "At SRC, everyone, including the clean-up crew, knows how to read our balance sheet. Everyone understands how he or she personally affects the income and profitability of the company. Each member of our team knows where we are in terms of our cash flow, how we generate it, and how we spend it." SRC spends 86% of its training budget on teaching everyone in the company how to be business people and not just hourly workers.

In the past, a leader was a boss. Today's leaders must be partners with their people…they no longer can lead solely based on positional power.

Ken Blanchard, business author and consultant

S.M.A.R.T. Goals

Almost all Business 101 professors use the acronym S.M.A.R.T. to teach their students how to set goals. The acronym is a helpful way to remember the most important components of a properly written goal.

A S.M.A.R.T. goal is:

- Specific – with the "who" and "why" clearly stated.
- Measurable – quantifiable and objective, not qualitative and subjective.
- Action-Oriented – with the "what" and "how" clearly identified.
- Realistic – honestly achievable, not simply a product of wishful thinking.
- Time-Framed – when to begin the task and when to expect completion are clearly stated.

All goals have a greater likelihood of success if they are more **Specific** than general, more **Measurable** than vague, more **Action-Oriented** than theoretical, more **Realistic** than hopeful, and bracketed by a beginning and ending **Time Frame**.

Here are four basic goals written by students prior to learning S.M.A.R.T. techniques and then reworded by the same students using the S.M.A.R.T. template.

Goal 1 (Before S.M.A.R.T.): My goal is to lose enough weight to fit into last summer's swimsuit.

Goal 1 (After S.M.A.R.T.): My goal is to fit into last year's swimsuit by losing at least 10 pounds, by walking two miles a day, three days a week, for four months starting this Tuesday. I will purchase a new scale by Saturday to measure my progress each week during the four months.

Goal 2 (Before S.M.A.R.T.): My goal is to become a better reader and to read more.

Goal 2 (After S.M.A.R.T.): My goal is to increase the amount of reading I do by reading at least one book every two months, beginning March 1 of this year. I will also join the Book Club at my neighborhood library next month to improve my retention and reading comprehension.

Goal 3 (Before S.M.A.R.T.): Our goal is to reduce the amount of employee turnover.

Goal 3 (After S.M.A.R.T.): Our goal is to reduce employee turnover by 27%. Beginning on January 1, we will be performing three reference checks per candidate, and we will increase the orientation/training time for all new employees from 10 hours to 24 hours. Seven of the additional hours will be spent "shadowing" an experienced associate.

Goal 4 (Before S.M.A.R.T.): My goal is to improve customer service in my department.

Goal 4 (After S.M.A.R.T.): My goal is to improve customer service by instituting a two-part customer feedback system. Part One will be in place by September 1 and will involve the establishment of a suggestion box at all entrances/exits. Part Two will be implemented by February 1 and will involve the creation of a Customer Advisory Panel that will meet for two hours twice a year.

Although these S.M.A.R.T. goals may require even more specific detailing to be considered complete, it's readily apparent that the "Before" Goals are underdeveloped and have little chance of success because there are no quantifiable methods to measure their outcomes.

Learn to write S.M.A.R.T. goals for yourself and with your people. You'll find that you and your team will become infinitely more accomplished.

To create a culture of commitment and accountability, the leader needs to know and be willing to share the organization's key performance indicators.

Genuine Leader

SUMMARY SCORE:

It's time to quantify how well you Know the Numbers that direct your business.

Are you a thoroughly informed leader who knows the numbers, manages the numbers, and shares them with your staff? Or are you a leader with little regard for personal accountability who manages by gut and allows others in your organization to do the same?

Score yourself on a scale of 1-10

Recommendations to Raise Your *Knows the Numbers* Score:

1. Enroll in a business math class or a basic finance course at your local community college.

As with public speaking, the more you immerse yourself in the field, the more comfortable and proficient you'll become in working with and understanding the numbers that are important to your business.

2. Adopt a tutor.

If you don't have access to a formal educational institution, ask a qualified member of your organization to tutor you. This way you will learn exactly what you need for your job without the extra topics taught in a business course.

3. Create a simple test to assess the "numbers knowledge" of your people.

Everybody in the company, not just the leader, needs to know the numbers. You and your people must be able to communicate using the same "numbers" language.

4. What's your goal for today?

Occasionally ask your managers what their goals are for the day. Listen for the response. Are their goals specific and quantifiable, or are they vague and general? Genuine Leaders develop specific, measurable goals, and they train their associates to do the same.

5. Use numbers to clarify your instructions.

Remember Parkinson's Law: work tends to fill the time allocated to it. If you give a directive without a time parameter, the time it takes to complete the task will vary wildly. When we fail to use our numbers to give direction, we miss a great opportunity to be more clear and concise. We can't blame our associates for our own failure to utilize numbers to clarify directives.

6. Use numbers in place of Weasel Words.

Don't say, "Please have most of this done by the end of the week." Instead, say, "Please have 95% of this done by Friday at 5:00 p.m."

7. Learn to utilize Excel spreadsheets.

Have someone in your office help you or use the Excel tutorial as an aid to better analyze the key numbers that are you are responsible for. Excel software allows you to organize a multitude of random numbers into a story, just as random words are organized to create a book.

RECOMMENDED READING

➡ Managing by the Numbers: A Commonsense Guide to Understanding and Using Your Company's Financials: An Essential Resource for Growing Businesses

by Chuck Kremer, Ron Rizzuto, and John Case *(Perseus Book Group, 2000)*

➡ The Great Game of Business

by Jack Stack *(Currency, 1994)*

➡ Open-Book Management: Developing Employees' Business Sense

by Jim Bado *(Crisp Learning, 1997)*

Chapter Four Appendix:

PROJECT TO IMPROVE PROFIT (P.I.P.) WORKSHEET

Use this worksheet to organize your projects, major promotions and sales events, and any other ideas which require capital expenditures. Remember, you are competing for precious capital expenditure dollars and must convince yourself and your organization that the projected Rate of Return on this project is high enough to justify the investment.

1. **Name of Project:**   Popcorn Machine
2. **Project Description:**   Install a popcorn machine near the lobby.

> The preparation of freshly popped, highly-aromatic popcorn will stimulate customers' senses and encourage them to stay in the store longer, adding to their purchasing time.
> Popcorn will be sold in small and medium-sized bags at prices of 25¢ and 50¢, respectively.

3. **Project Dates:**   Start Date: June 1
                             Completion Date: July 15
4. **Elements of Expense**
   (Break down your idea or project into the various elements that together constitute your total plan. For example, consider the construction phase, equipment required, electrical/plumbing, and inventory startup.)

Elements of Expense	Est. Cost	Start & Stop Dates
Purchase of Popcorn Machine, Model 189	$ 789	Order & Delivery by July 2
Purchase of Wheeled Cart for Machine	$ 669	Order & Delivery by July 2
Installation of 220v & 110v electric lines	$ 350	Start on June 2, Finish July 3
Initial inventory of popcorn and supplies	$ 229	Order & Delivery by July 3
Miscellaneous Expenses	$ 129	Period of June 1 to July 15
Projected Cost:	**$2,166**	

(Have you included all the costs? Can you defend each expense?)

5. Calculate Rate of Return

(This section is used to project sales or revenues, operating costs and net profits in determining an average Rate of Return for a three-year period. Take care in preparing your estimates, as you may need to defend them now and in the future.)

Projections	Year 1	Year 2	Year 3
Sales	$8,000	$8,300	$8,700
Operating Expenses	$7,250	$7,365	$7,579
Depreciation	$480	$480	$480
Net Income (Before Taxes)	$270	$455	$641

The Rate of Return formula is:

$$\frac{\text{Project's Average Annual After-Tax Net Income}}{\text{Average Investment Cost + Salvage Value}}$$

Step 1 – Calculate the average **Net Income Before Taxes** from the chart above:
$$\frac{\$270 + \$455 + \$641}{3} = \$455$$

Step 2 – Multiply the **average Net Income** by 100% minus the company's income tax rate (33%)
$$\$455 \times 67\% = \$304.85$$

Step 3 – Calculate average **Investment Cost** by using the total from Item 4 of Estimated Project Cost and adding any **Salvage Value** to it.
$$\frac{\$2,166 + \$400}{3} = \$855.33$$

Step 4 – The final step is to divide average **Net Income After Taxes** by **Average Investment Cost**:
$$\frac{\$304.85}{\$855.33} = 35.6\% \text{ Rate of Return}$$

6. Submit P.I.P. Report to Your Supervisor

You will be notified, within 30 days from the date of submission, if and when we plan to proceed with your project.

CHAPTER 5

GENUINE LEADERS ARE UNQUESTIONABLY HONEST

Honesty is the first chapter in the book of wisdom.

Thomas Jefferson, American president

In court, we are reminded to "tell the truth, the whole truth, and nothing but the truth." The Bible tells us, "Honesty makes a good person's life easier." And from day one, our parents threatened to wash our mouths out with a bar of soap if we ever told a lie.

Why, then, do some surveys report as many as 93% of Americans admit to lying regularly at work? This is a disturbing statistic that we should all work to change.

In many circles, it's taken for granted that lying is a necessary part of business. In 1998, a now very visible corporate leader gave an interview to *Fast Company* magazine. He said, "Let's be honest: we lie, and our colleagues lie to us. That's how human beings operate. People prefer to tell other people what they want to hear. I don't worry very much about whether everything I hear in a meeting or read in an e-mail is the unvarnished truth. I don't need perfect people. I need successful people – people who can think for themselves and get the job done. And if they need to tell a little white lie once in a while, well, I can live with that."

That corporate leader was Mark Cuban, the owner of the Dallas Mavericks. He was the co-founder of MicroSolutions, which he sold to CompuServe. When he spoke to *Fast Company*, he was getting ready to sell another company that he had co-founded, Broadcast.com, which provided multimedia and streaming on the Internet. He's a heavy hitter, an extremely successful executive – and a proponent of lying.

Compare Mark Cuban's words to those of George Washington: "I hope I shall possess firmness and virtue enough to maintain what I consider the most enviable of all titles, the character of an honest man." While the legend of George Washington and the ill-fated cherry tree may be a myth, our nation's first great leader is still historically equated with honesty.

And then there's our 16th president, who was so well known for his ethical stance that he was called "Honest Abe." Lincoln based his whole career on his reputation for telling the truth. As he put it, "I have always wanted to deal with everyone I meet candidly and honestly. If I have made any assertion not warranted by the facts, and it is pointed out to me, I will withdraw cheerfully." How many of today's politicians would embrace that philosophy?

When organizational leaders such as Mark Cuban think that lying and dishonesty are "the way human beings operate," it's no wonder lying has become so pervasive in today's business environment. Almost without exception, the company's culture reflects the person at the helm. If the CEO freely admits to lying and accepting lies, it won't be long before the organization will be awash in dishonesty.

I strongly believe that successful corporate leaders who accept lying as a cost of doing business are in the minority. People like Mary Kay Ash, the founder of Mary Kay Cosmetics, are more prevalent among successful leaders. She said, "Honesty is the cornerstone of all success, without which confidence and the ability to perform shall cease to exist." John F. Dodge, who founded one of Detroit's automotive dynasties with his brother Horace, said, "There is no twilight zone of honesty in business. A thing is right or it's wrong. It's black or it's white." Firestone Tire and Rubber Company founder, Harvey Firestone, believed that "fundamental honesty is the keystone of business."

A firm commitment to honesty is what we need if we are to build the ethical and moral backbone that's the hallmark of a well-run organization. And it all starts with you becoming the honest leader you need to be.

"Expose the truth, own it, and then act on it."

Bob Stapleton, senior vice-president, Food Lion

Honesty and Integrity...What's the Difference?

When I decided to write this book on leadership, I knew that it had to include a chapter on honesty, especially in light of the numerous recent business debacles that have been traced back to lying at the highest levels. In the course of my research, I quickly found that most of us tend to use the words *integrity* and *honesty* interchangeably. To find out the difference between their definitions, I took a trip to the Internet. First, I found it interesting that the most often searched for word on the Merriam-Webster site (www.m-w.com) is *integrity*. If 93% of Americans admit to lying, where does our fascination with "integrity" come from? Maybe people are searching for "integrity" because deep down they are ashamed of lying.

Checking *integrity*, I found that it meant "uprightness of character; honesty; probity." *Honesty* was defined as "the quality of being honest; uprightness of character, conduct etc., integrity."

The two definitions were pretty close to identical, which made me feel better about using them interchangeably all these years. But what about that word *probity*? I couldn't recall ever seeing this word before, let alone having used it. *Probity*, it turns out, is a noun that means "virtue or integrity **tested and confirmed**, strict honesty [emphasis added]." Whoa, that's powerful! "Integrity, tested and confirmed," sounds like the next level up on the honesty scale. To have been tested and confirmed as honest seems much more accomplished than simply being honest. It's like moving up the ladder from good to great, from smart to genius, from honesty to probity.

I found it interesting that the word probity is so rarely used in comparison with honesty and integrity. Maybe it's because the quality of "confirmed honesty" is so rare. Probity is a word we can use when talking about Cynthia Cooper, WorldCom Inc.'s internal auditor who uncovered one of the largest accounting frauds in history. In 2002, *Time* magazine named her as a Person of the Year. Time's other honored whistleblowers were Sherron Watkins, the former vice-president of Enron who exposed the accounting issues that would bring down the company, and Coleen Rowley, the FBI counsel whose memo caused a complete reorganization at the Bureau. These three leaders were singled out for international acclaim, not because of their indisputable business abilities, but simply for telling the truth.

They say honesty pays, but as American humorist Kin Hubbard said, "Honesty...doesn't seem to pay enough to suit some people." Even the Reverend Billy Graham admitted that "everybody has a little bit of Watergate in him." Although it may seem difficult to achieve, your ultimate goal must be to become someone with a reputation for probity.

In this book, I've decided to use integrity to define a person's internal ethics. Just as you can be "self-made" or have "self-worth," I'll use integrity in the sense of being "self-honest." In contrast, I'll use honesty to describe how a person interacts with others. Thus, we have internal integrity and external honesty.

Finally, I'll use the word probity as the Holy Grail. A leader who demonstrates true probity has achieved the ultimate goal of having total, unwavering honesty and integrity, both personally and professionally.

With these definitions in tow, let's begin.

Degrees of Honesty?

Honesty is one of the few words that shouldn't need a preceding modifier, yet some people are compelled to use "almost" or "truly" or "totally" when talking about being honest. Why? I can't see how there can be any variation. You can't be almost honest or pretty honest any more than you can be a little pregnant. You're either honest or you're not. It's that simple.

Unfortunately, our society has accepted and even encouraged the notion that there can be variations of honesty. We've gone so far as to invent words to replace "honesty" so that we can be politically correct and soothe the ruffled feathers of the dishonest. No one "lies" today; instead, people "compromise their principles" or "have misguided values." We never hear that "their lying and cheating destroyed the company."

But argue as I might that honesty is a yes-or-no, black-or-white, guilty-or-not-guilty situation, the idea of varying degrees of honesty has been indelibly ingrained in our society. In an effort to take a more open-minded look at this idea, I've identified six degrees of honesty. It's easy for any one of us to fall into a lower-level degree at some time or other, but I'd argue that once we cross the line from unquestionably honest to basically honest, we've compromised our integrity and cannot be a person of true probity.

THE SIX DEGREES OF HONESTY

1st Degree – Probity/Unquestionably Honest

This person is not only honest, but has been proven, tested and confirmed as authentically honest. Actions, not just words, have validated this person's commitment to being honest.

Probity is a great quality in leaders, but it can be found in all types of people. For instance, I decided to call my local Culligan Man for a system check-up because our house water system was 13 years old.

When I got off the phone, I thought about what I had just done. Essentially, I'd called a water treatment company to advise me on whether to spend an unspecified amount of money on a problem that didn't exist. That's when I realized the powerful difference between *Caveat Emptor* (let the buyer beware) and a true fiduciary relationship. We've all been lied to, cheated, and misled by unscrupulous salespeople whose only purpose was to separate us from our money. The people at this Culligan franchise, however, never seem to be after the quick buck. They're focused on the long haul, believing that in the end, many more dollars will flow from a relationship built on honesty and fair dealing than from a backstabbing, double-crossing relationship that is liable to fall apart at any moment.

When Jim, the Culligan service technician, arrived on time as usual, he proceeded to perform his routine service exam. I asked if there were a better, more elaborate system I should consider or if there were any new chemicals or attachments I should be using. He said that my system was still the best out there and that the newest model was computer-driven versus gear-driven but

lambasted me for criticizing her after all the years she had given to the company.

Apparently, throughout her entire fifteen-year relationship with the company, no one had ever leveled with Madeline. Her hot-blooded reputation was so well known that no supervisor ever dared to be brutally honest with her performance issues. Instead, they would throw a few bucks her way in the form of a raise to appease her.

After her outburst, Madeline grabbed her papers and literally stormed out of the building. Some people might have considered her behavior unforgivable and taken her departure as a form of resignation. But I knew that Madeline was an asset to us and deserved to be guided so that she could become even more valuable.

I gave her a few days to cool down, then called to ask her forgiveness for our failure to level with her in the past. I asked her to allow us to help improve her career with a sincere, honest performance review process. Fortunately, Madeline accepted my apology and agreed to come back.

What stuck with me from this situation was the negative power of not leveling and of not telling the truth. Because her supervisors hadn't been brutally honest with Madeline in previous performance reviews, she had stopped growing and had developed a serious ego issue. Madeline was a valuable manager who, if directed positively, could yield significant results for the company over the years. Instead, we almost ruined her.

You're often asked to respond to questions of honesty both in business and in your personal life. If you can be brutally honest without being mean, your leveling with people will be a positive force in their lives.

> ## Be who you are and say what you feel
> ## because those who mind don't matter
> ## and those who matter don't mind.
>
> *Theodor Geisel ("Dr. Seuss"), American children's author*

3rd Degree – Basically Honest

Basically honest people will occasionally lie in social situations. They might tell a parent that his or her painfully homely child is adorable, refuse a party invitation because they had a previous (non-existent) commitment, or assure their 300-pound boss that his new green plaid suit looks great. These are the social lies that most people tell without giving them much thought. I never thought that this type of lying was a big deal until I met Barbara.

I had always considered myself to be a perfectly honest person, but it wasn't until I was 24 and hired my first secretary that I realized what a social liar I had become.

That day, that phone call, that moment of revelation is as clear to me today as it was 30 years ago. I was at my desk when the first call of the day came in and the intercom light came on. I pushed Barbara's extension. She had only been with me for a few days, but Barbara had already proven herself to be a jewel. She had been a standout in the parade of applicants. When her interview was over, I cancelled all the remaining interviews, letting them know that the position was filled. Barbara had poise, intelligence, maturity, initiative, and impeccable references.

This particular morning, Barbara told me that a Mr. Nichols was on the line. Mr. Nichols was a real estate agent pestering me to buy a piece of property that I had no interest in buying.

My immediate response to Barbara was to tell Mr. Nichols that I wasn't in. Instead of Barbara's normally quick reply, there was dead silence. "Barbara?" I said, "Barbara, are you still there?"

The long silence on her end was finally broken. "Yes, I'm here, but I can't say that." "You can't say what?" I asked.

"Harold," she said, "I can't tell Mr. Nichols that you're not in because you are." Barbara's silence to my initial directive had evidently given her time to decide how she was going to tell her new boss that she wasn't about to lie for him. Even in this relatively harmless situation, she refused to compromise her personal values.

My first reaction to her statement was, "That's what I get for hiring a minister's wife." My next, more appropriate, thought was, "How many other associates have I solicited to be accessories to my dishonest acts?" Ministers' wives weren't the only people who were adamant about not lying for themselves or anyone else.

Since that memorable morning, I've figured out how to say "no" to an annoying caller without lying, how to get out of something by telling the truth instead of fabricating a story, and how to be upfront with people. Now, social lying seems unnecessary, unprofessional, and wrong.

4th Degree – The Spin Doctors

These "white liars" spin the facts. Deceptive practices are a spin doctor's bread-and-butter. Typically, spin doctors have no criminal intent. They manipulate situations to protect their reputations, to stay out of trouble, or to deflect blame. They could be professionals – defense attorneys, public relations experts, personal agents, advertising copywriters, etc. – who are paid to take bad situations or inferior products and put a positive spin on them for the sake of their clients.

The tabloids have taken spinning to its worst extreme. They can take a whiff of truth and spew out a cloud of lies and innuendo. Companies do the same thing when they take the numbers and spin a story that bears little relation to truth, citing statistics as proof of veracity. But as Mark Twain wrote, "There are three kinds of lies – lies, damn lies, and statistics."

Spinning the truth can start early in life. When I was eight, my little brother and I found my parents' secret stash of Christmas gifts. Grabbing the biggest package, Jeffrey and I opened two sets of cowboy holsters stuffed with shiny silver guns. They were incredible – exactly what we had asked from Santa.

Unfortunately for us, my mother remembered how she had left the packages stacked in the closet. When she confronted us, asking, "Who was in the closet?" I began my spin by responding, "We were, but we didn't see the pistols." My mother reacted by donating the pistols to a local charity.

At the time, losing those holsters was the worst moment of my young life. But in hindsight, the episode gave me the best lesson I've ever learned about the importance of telling the truth. Immediately after being trapped in my lie, my mother told Jeffrey and me that had we "'fessed up" to our venture into her closet, she would have given us the treasured pistols at Christmas as planned. If you lie, we learned, you lose.

In almost any organization, a leader will inevitably be called upon to give a reference for someone who isn't qualified enough to be recommended without reservation. There are many restrictions that open us up to lawsuits if we say anything negative, so we often find ourselves trapped. In those situations, we must make a choice: Do we tell a boldfaced lie, or do we tell the truth with a spin?

"Spinners" know the versatility of the English language. Language guru Richard Lederer, writing in the *Mensa Review*, addresses this issue by showing how to give carefully worded statements about a candidate's suitability without lying.

For instance, if tardiness is an issue, Lederer suggests that you say, "A man like him is hard to find" – never mind if this is because he's never in the office. Lederer goes on to quote a number of two-sided statements taken from Robert Thorton's Lexicon of Intentionally Ambiguous Recommendations. These statements include the following:

"I can't say enough good things about her."

"He will take full advantage of his staff."

"She takes a lot of enjoyment out of her work."

"His input was always critical."

"To get the job done, we need 10 employees like him."

You get the idea. In cases like these, artfully spinning the truth may keep you from getting sued.

The dark side of dealing with "spin doctors" is that you never know when they will slide down to the next degree of deception. It's a slippery slope. As they become more comfortable "spinning," they'll become more comfortable with the 5th Degree of Honesty, which is simply deceit.

5th Degree – The Dishonest Person

The dishonest person knows the laws and wouldn't consider breaking them, but would lie or cheat for personal gain or to avoid getting into trouble without giving it a second thought. The dishonest person doesn't consider lying or cheating to be personal affronts – they're just necessary parts of business and of life. Typically, these liars are surprised that the person whom they've cheated is so offended.

Beginning in childhood, we get mixed signals about honesty. As a kid, I loved baseball. I played almost every day in the summer. One day, I was substituting for our absent centerfielder. It was late in the game and we were leading by two runs. There were two outs and runners on first and second. The batter at the plate took a full swing and sent a pitch screaming between me and the right fielder. I ran as fast as my little legs could take me, leaped spread-eagled toward the outfield fence, and stabbed the ball backhanded with my glove. I immediately heard my right fielder say "Great catch!" and I thought I heard someone yell, "Out!"

While this moment seemed to be developing into the greatest sports memory I would ever have, it turned awful in an instant. The ball had wedged itself in my groping glove, but as I landed on the outfield grass, I found the ball loose on the ground, cradled next to my stomach.

With my back to the umpire and the infield, and no one beyond the outfield fence to witness the play, I was momentarily alone with the fact I had dropped the ball. This was the biggest ethical dilemma of my young life: should I fake the catch and be a hero, or should I tell the truth?

With two outs, the runners were moving with the hit, and I had to make a split-second decision. Jumping to my feet, I fired the ball to the cut-off man, who looked bewildered. He, in turn, relayed the throw home, holding the batter on second and one of the two runners on third.

Unfortunately, I received no praise for telling the truth. In fact, my coach yelled at me for admitting that the ball had hit the ground, since everyone in the park, including the umpire, thought that I'd caught the ball. The lesson my coach wanted me to learn was, "If no one sees you cheat, it's okay. Keep your mouth shut."

Leaders also wear coaches' caps and have a responsibility to teach their followers the difference between right and wrong. But on that memorable day as a Little Leaguer, the lesson I learned about honesty had to be self-taught.

6th Degree – The Criminally Dishonest

Criminally dishonest people think nothing of lying, cheating, and stealing in flagrant disobedience of the law. Whether they run a company or a gang of thieves, these people think that laws were made for other folks. The criminally dishonest think that they are immune to any rules and regulations.

I lived my life in a certain way to make sure that I would never violate any law… certainly never any criminal laws…and always maintained that most important to me was my integrity, was my character, were my values.

Kenneth Lay, former chairman of Enron

While on a family vacation, I began to read The Daily Update, our hotel's news roundup. The paper was the hotel's way of condensing all the important news from around the world into a quick summary.

The headline "An Executive's Fatal Flaw" and the subsequent article caught my eye and my ire.

> *The tragedy of the former Enron chairman Kenneth L. Lay, who died Wednesday of a heart attack at the age of 64, is not that his name will always be linked to the seminal business scandal of the era. Nor is it that his fall from grace was so precipitous.*

> *No, the tragedy of Ken Lay is that, right up until the end, he never fully understood what he'd done wrong or his own considerable culpability in his company's demise.*

So far, I'm in full agreement with the writer. But the closing two paragraphs drove me crazy.

> *Thanks in large part to Enron and Lay, much has changed in corporate America. Boards are under far more scrutiny than they used to be.*

> *But there are some things you can't legislate, or teach in business school.* ***Sound business judgment*** *[emphasis added] is one of those things. Sad to say, that's what Lay lacked most of all.*

Is it really "sound business judgment" that Ken Lay lacked? Since when had lying, cheating, and blatant deception become merely "unsound business judgment?" I always thought that "business judgment" allowed leaders to determine how much to spend, whom to promote, or what product to create. Not telling the truth, deceiving loyal stockholders, and destroying the financial futures of your loyal staff were, to me, errors of a far graver magnitude than just poor business decisions.

Pretenders may forgive a lie as "unsound business judgment," but Genuine Leaders are unquestionably honest. Period.

I played by the rules of politics as I found them.

Richard M. Nixon, American president

A Final Thought Regarding Honesty

Dishonesty is a chronic disease, degenerative for the perpetrator and the organization as a whole. Telling the truth is empowering. It's regenerative. It builds confidence, trust, relationships, and strong organizations.

I was disappointed to see the following on the marquee in front of my son's middle school:

"This month's word is Honesty."

Therein lies the problem in our society and in business today. "Honesty" is not an occasional fad. You can't be "really honest" in October and "not very honest" in November. Honesty must exist everyday and forever throughout your organization.

SUMMARY SCORE:

Evaluate yourself on your personal integrity and honesty toward others. No one but you need ever see this score. Fill in a number between 1 and 10 in the square below.

Recommendations to Raise Your *Honesty* Score:

1. Determine how accustomed you've become to fibbing.

You might find it embarrassing. Remember how Barbara affected me? Then tell one less lie per day, per week, or per month, depending on how often your fibs fly now. By doing this, over time, your habit of telling lies, regardless of their size and frequency, will be whittled down to nothing.

2. Make a pact.

Extend honesty into all facets of your life. Explicitly ask your children, as early in their life as possible, never to lie to you or to anyone else. Then assure them that when they do tell you the truth, you'll never yell at them or punish them for their transgressions. It's an incredible pact to form with your children. And it works. Let me tell you about Alex and the golf ball.

I'm extremely proud of my children because of their upstanding and honorable characters. I've heard dozens of parents say, "Wait until your kids become teenagers – telling lies will become a way of life." An annual online survey of 787 young people ages 13-18 was commissioned by the financial services firm Deloitte & Touche and by Junior Achievement Worldwide, which offers school programs on citizenship, business, and ethics. In the survey conducted by Harris Interactive, teens were asked about their actions in the past year. Sadly, 69% said they had lied regularly.

From the very beginning, my wife and I agreed that we would never lie to our children no matter what, and when they became old enough to understand our commitment to them, we would ask that they never lie to us. Additionally, when they told the truth, we would never be mad or punish them for their wrongdoing.

When Alex was six years old, he could swing a golf club as if he had played many times before. He was allowed to hit golf balls toward the woods in the back yard, but we warned him not to aim anywhere near our little barn with its large glass windows. One time, Alex accidentally hit a shot that landed on the roof of the barn. The ball landed with a loud boom, and he thought that the sound was pretty cool. I saw the thrill in his eyes and thought it prudent to steer him away from the barn.

One afternoon, Alex came to the back door of our house all red-eyed and tearful. As I opened the door, he cried, "Dad, I broke one of the windows in the barn." As he sobbed out his explanation of what happened, I instinctively held my son close. When he finished, I looked him in the eyes and told him how proud I was that he told us the truth. He could have made up a story about a bird hitting the window or that the neighbor's kid had done it. Instead, he told us exactly what happened, which made my wife and I very proud. I reminded him of our agreement that his mom and I would never be mad at him, no matter what he did, when he told the truth. He replied, "Thanks, Dad. I love you." I would have never guessed that a broken window could turn into a great day for us as parents and a great day in the development of our son as a good person.

3. Live the two rules of 21st century leadership.

I was fortunate to attend a conference where General Norman Schwarzkopf was the keynote presenter. I'll never forget his closing remarks. He said, "Here are the two rules of 21st century leadership. One: When placed in command, take charge. Two: Do what's right."

Great advice to live by. Doing the right thing can have a price, but it's a price worth paying.

My first major decision as CEO of a retail group was to switch wholesale suppliers. I was only two years out of graduate school and remarkably inexperienced; however, I saw the decision to switch as straightforward. The comparison between our existing supplier and the alternative favored the new supplier by a wide margin.

The morning after receiving our first delivery from the new company, I anxiously asked the grocery manager and the store manager how the order had been picked, shipped, and received. They responded that the order was received in excellent physical condition. Then, with a smile, the grocery manager said, "We even got a free pallet of tuna fish." Apparently, on our new supplier's first delivery, the company had mispicked and sent a pallet of tuna fish in place of the pallet of cat food we had ordered.

To this day, I remember the grocery manager's smile as he calculated the profit he'd make because of the mistake. I also remember his disbelief when I told him to notify our new supplier about the error and to offer them the opportunity to rectify it. I made sure that all of the associates who knew about this error were aware of our decision to correct the discrepancy even though we could make a small profit by letting the mistake slide. I knew that my management team and retail associates had to do the right thing. Just as I'd learned in Little League, honesty is always the best policy.

To this day, I'm convinced that some suppliers purposely send an order through with an error in the customer's favor so that they can test the honesty of their new customer. Indeed, on two other occasions in my career, a switch to a new supplier has resulted in a delivery with an error resulting in a profit windfall for me. In each incident, I responded honestly and made sure that everyone involved was aware of our decision to do the right thing. After these incidents, my company always seemed to enjoy stronger relationships with our suppliers. We were rarely, if ever, challenged when we discovered that we had been inadvertently shorted on a shipment.

4. Give the Spending Allowance Test.

A technique you can use to assess an individual's integrity inclinations is what I call the Spending Allowance Test. The idea is to offer an unproven member of your team a spending allowance, which he or she can then use on an upcoming assignment that involves travel. You can use this test on someone who's new to the company, new to management, or ready for advancement. Offer a substantial sum – for example, $250 cash with few strings attached. You can say, "This money should cover your incidental expenses," or, "Charge what you can to the corporate credit card and use this for everything else." Be as vague as you can, especially about what to do with any remaining funds. While you're not trying to trap the employee, the test is simply a way to see where he or she stands in regard to fair play, accountability, good sense, and integrity.

In my experience, this Spending Allowance Test generates a wide variety of results. Someone may return with every receipt and every cent accounted for. Someone may later admit to using some of the funds for a needed haircut. Someone may make a late car payment with unused funds, justifying it by claiming that the business trip caused him or her to miss the due date.

It's very difficult to determine someone's inclination to stray from the ideal standard of honesty. This test allows a sneak peek into the mind of someone on your team who's in a responsible position. You'll find out that given enough rope, some will hang themselves.

5. Ask effective interview questions.

One of the best interview questions I have ever used, one that specifically addresses the candidate's integrity, is, "What might I find in your personal history that few people know and that would really surprise me if or when I do a thorough and legal background check on you?"

After asking this question, I carefully watch the candidates as they try to guess whether or not I would really do a thorough check and how much they should admit to. More often than not, candidates offer much more than I would have ever been able to learn on my own.

Always do right.
This will gratify some and astonish the rest.

Mark Twain, American author

RECOMMENDED READING

➠ Principle-Centered Leadership
by Steven R. Covey *(Free Press, 1992)*

➠ Absolute Honesty: Building a Corporate Culture That Values
Straight Talk and Rewards Integrity
by Larry Johnson and Bob Phillips *(AMACOM, 2003)*

➠ Integrity Works: Strategies for Becoming a Trusted, Respected and
Admired Leader
by Dana Telford and Adrian Gostick *(Gibbs Smith, 2005)*

CHAPTER 6

GENUINE LEADERS
DISCONTINUE THINGS

If at first you don't succeed, try again.
Then quit.
There's no use being a damn fool about it.

W. C. Fields, American actor

The Cycle of Success

While it's been said that "success breeds success," I don't believe the formula is that simple. Instead, it's more accurate to say that success breeds complacency. Complacency then breeds failure. And only through an organization's effort to refocus and recommit can success return. Here's my circular reasoning.

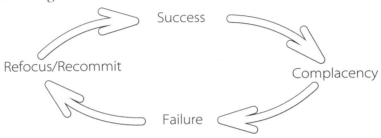

There are thousands of proverbs about the importance of failing and learning from those failures. For example, "It's not how far you fall, but how high you bounce back," "It's better to have tried and failed than never to have tried at all," "Failure is the fertilizer of success" – on and on they go. Unfortunately, Pretenders can't admit to failure, so they rarely learn from it. Genuine Leaders know that failing is often a necessary part of the process of achieving success. Although they detest failure, Genuine Leaders embrace it and grow stronger from the experience. They refocus and recommit, which ultimately leads to future success.

It's essential for aspiring leaders to understand the following truth: Every strategy, sooner or later, begins to fail. And when something begins to fail, it must be altered or discontinued.

Often, leaders find it especially difficult to discontinue something that they've personally created. Ego, pride, the time and money invested, and the stigma of failing contribute to the reluctance to end a project. Leaders will opt to continue the status quo, hoping that the passing of time will rectify their problem.

Part of being a winner is knowing when enough is enough. Sometimes you have to give up the fight and walk away, and move on to something that's more productive.

Donald Trump, American businessman

One way to decide if something should be discontinued is to use a T-Bar Analysis, which is a simple comparison of a decision's pluses and minuses. Assign a value from 1 to 10 to each plus or minus entry that represents the relative importance of each. When you look at side-by-side numerical comparison of each pro and con, you can make a better, more objective decision. Here are two examples of T-Bar Analyses:

Example 1: **Should we buy new uniforms now or wait one more year?**

(+)	(-)
Improved public image.....................7	Expense of uniforms 8
Increased team morale 9	Time spent securing donations...............3
Improved recruiting chances for next season 5	Forgo other needed equipment (Opportunity cost)...................................4
Total 21	Total 15

Conclusion: Buy the uniforms

Example 2: **Should we have a company picnic?**

(+)	(-)
Employee morale builder 9	Payroll hours to prepare 7
Improved management/employee communication 9	$$ expense for food and prizes 4
Employee/family connection 7	Legal liability in case of accident 9
Part of our Strategic Plan 5	
Better vendor relations (vendors also invited) 5	
Improved part-timer and full-timer interaction 6	
Total 41	Total 20

Conclusion: Have the picnic

Throughout their careers, Genuine Leaders must choose to discontinue **physical assets,** such as a piece of property that has to be sold; **company policies** that have to be updated; **operating procedures** that should be re-evaluated; and **people (associates)** who need to be terminated. Let's look at examples of each.

1. Discontinuing Physical Assets

The "Project to Improve Performance" (P.I.P.) worksheet at the end of Chapter Four is designed to determine an investment's financial viability before it is bought or built. But what happens if a performing asset turns into a non-performing asset? One obvious option is to discontinue it.

In Chapter Four, we saw the example of selling one's original headquarters office as an emotional decision. But armed with the salient numbers, a Genuine Leader can cut through the emotions and make the right call.

Genuine Leaders are able to make these difficult decisions when Pretenders can't, because Genuine Leaders can connect the Mission Statement, the Strategic Plan, and the Critical Number Indicators in their thought processes. Genuine Leaders can visualize how the elimination of an asset, policy, procedure, or employee can benefit the organization as a whole in the long run. They aren't held back by the lesser implications.

In the 1970s, Pepsi unleashed its "Pepsi Challenge" campaign, claiming that in blind tests, consumers preferred Pepsi to other colas. Market research showed that many customers liked the "sweeter" taste that Pepsi offered. Pepsi was steadily gaining market share, and the Coca-Cola Company, its major rival, became worried.

In response to Pepsi's success, Coca-Cola developed and test-marketed a sweeter, higher-fructose syrup and test-marketed it. The results were overwhelming. Many consumers preferred the new formula to both Coke and Pepsi. The testers were also asked if they would buy and drink the new formula should Coca-Cola choose to bring the product to market. Most consumers said that they would buy it. With these numbers backing the decision, New Coke was launched to replace the traditional Coke, which was pulled off the shelves.

The initial introduction of the product caused the company's stock to skyrocket. However, despite the early success, a grassroots consumer backlash began, mainly from southern consumers who perceived New Coke as surrendering to the Yankees. The Coca-Cola Company underestimated the public's emotional attachment to the traditional Coke product.

Humbled by the mistake, Coca-Cola re-introduced the original Coca-Cola formula to the market under the name Classic Coke. And in the end, Coca-Cola actually benefited from the error. By the end of the year Classic Coke was outselling both New Coke and Pepsi.

The Genuine Leaders at Coca-Cola Company went with the numbers. They recognized the threat from Pepsi and decided to counteract it. Unfortunately, the idea didn't have the success that they'd hoped for. But rather than stubbornly sticking with the new product, in less than three months Coca-Cola responded to the numbers and returned Classic Coke to the market.

A setback is the opportunity to begin again more intelligently.

Henry Ford, American industrialist

When I was planning my first restaurant, I noticed a flaw in the design of my prototype. One of the four corners of the dining area had no uniquely attractive feature near it. There was an ice cream fountain in one corner, a fireplace in another, a kids' center in the third, but the fourth corner was just dull. In fact, it sported an unattractive entrance to the kitchen.

The day that I recognized this flaw, I was in Las Vegas, surrounded by lights, bells, whistles, and Wheels of Fortune. I decided to put a customized Las Vegas-style Wheel of Fortune in that lonely corner of the restaurant and place a cuckoo clock next to it. The plan was to prepare one of our signature ice cream sundaes every hour when the cuckoo sounded. The manager on duty would spin the Wheel of Fortune. Each number on the wheel corresponded to a table in the restaurant. Then the manager would put the just-made sundae on a tray, parade it through the entire restaurant for all to see, and deliver it to the lucky table.

For less than $800, I had come up with a unique and exciting feature for the fourth corner of the restaurant. Everyone thought that the wheel would create lots of interest and excitement every hour.

Sadly, my creative idea turned out to be a dud for three unforeseen reasons. First, our opening month was rough. We made lots of mistakes and our food took too long to prepare. We found out people weren't thrilled at winning a free ice cream sundae after waiting 40 minutes for their hamburgers and fries. Second, during the busiest hours, the managers often failed to hear the cuckoo and didn't follow through with the sundae. Conversely, during slow afternoons when only two or three of the 45 tables in the restaurant were being used, the managers didn't know what to do. Should they listen for the cuckoo clock and hope the wheel landed on one of the few tables occupied, or should they ignore it completely?

After several weeks of trying to make the idea work, I retired the clock and the Wheel of Fortune. I could hear my managers' collective sigh of relief loud and clear.

Genuine Leaders discontinue things that no longer work or never worked. Naturally, I was disappointed that my idea had failed to generate the excitement that we had anticipated, but I recognized that it was time to move on to a better plan.

If you find yourself in a hole, the first thing to do is stop digging.

Will Rogers, American humorist

2. Discontinuing Policies

"Don't let it die; kill it first!" That's what I tell supervisors when I encourage them to discontinue policies that have been ignored, become antiquated, or don't make sense for our current operations. All too often, we let these outdated policies drift unnoticed in the back pages of our manuals. Problems arise when one manager decides to enforce something that other managers have ignored. Charges of discrimination, favoritism, and mismanagement arise from our failures to delete old policies from the pertinent rules and regulations.

Here are three actual company policies, clearly stated but loosely enforced, along with the real-life remarks I hear all too often.

Company Policy: *The hiring of family members in the same company, division or unit is strictly prohibited.*

Manager Reality: "But what if they work different shifts? What about our shortage of help? What about a cousin or an aunt? Who counts as a family member? You told us to search for the best and his brother is one of the best available."

Company Policy: *No refund without a receipt.*

Manager Reality: "But if the customer makes a big enough fuss, she'll get her receipt-less refund."

Company Policy: *Coming to work later than scheduled is a company policy infraction. Two tardy notices will yield a written disciplinary action.*
Manager Reality: "But she's a good employee and I'm short-handed. She stayed late for us a few times in the past and she was only five minutes late."

A Company Policy must be enforced as written in the policy manual. Otherwise, it should be edited for clarity and specificity, should be altered to suit the times, or should be eliminated.

In addition to confusion and frustration, there can be huge repercussions due to non-compliance or non-enforcement of an organization's policy, including government fines and lawsuits.

It's much more important to kill bad bills than to pass good ones.
Calvin Coolidge, American president

Believe it or not, one of my toughest fights as a business owner centered on a ketchup bottle. Many people wouldn't even notice it, but the ketchup bottle can be a rather unsightly condiment on a table in a restaurant. Our restaurant franchisor's policy specified the classic, old-fashioned Heinz clear glass bottle with the screw-off top. I favored the now ubiquitous squeezable red plastic model with the flip top design.

Even though the plastic bottle cost a few cents more, it always looked clean and full because of its red plastic container. It was consumer-friendly because it was squeezable. In addition, my preferred plastic bottle prevented the little-known but widespread industry practice of using a "ketchup cow." A ketchup cow is an apparatus that allows a restaurant to drain five or six almost empty ketchup bottles into one full bottle to save on food costs. I always thought the ketchup cow was a nasty and potentially dangerous food handling practice. Unlike the glass bottle, the cap on the plastic bottle could not be removed.

The point value of the pluses on my T-Bar Analysis for the plastic bottle was three times that of the minuses, but the biggest minus on the list is what ultimately tipped the scales in our favor. This minus referenced a young boy who took a knife from his plate, licked off some mashed potatoes, and inserted the blade into the old glass bottle to start the ketchup flowing. This graphic visual finally convinced the franchisor that glass bottles were perhaps not the best way to go. Let's see the T-Bar Analysis.

Example 3: Glass Ketchup Bottles vs. Squeezable Plastic with Flip Tops

(+)	(-)
Huge inventory on hand 2	Customer contamination potential 10
Less expensive than plastic 10	Unsanitary product consolidation 8
Server familiarity 1	Higher waste factor.......................................3 (Ketchup left in bottle)
	Glass breakage hazard 5
	Service disadvantage when compared..........6 to competitors who have plastic
	Caps get misplaced 2
	Looks unsightly when almost empty............5
Total 13	Total 39

Conclusion: Discontinue using glass ketchup bottles

Genuine Leaders use a T-Bar style analysis to look at the pros and cons of a decision and demand a discontinuation if the minuses outweigh the pluses. Pretenders, on the other hand, hang on to bad policies too long because they are too stubborn, proud, or unwilling to take the initiative and make the change.

3. Discontinuing Procedures

When old procedures are allowed to remain in place too long, they become bad habits that get harder to break over time.

A dear friend and colleague, Murray Raphel of Raphel Marketing, shared the following story with me. It's a classic example of implementing perfectly valid procedures at an appropriate time and place but never failing to alter or eliminate them when they have been rendered obsolete.

During World War II, an American general was doing air surveillance over some British artillery units. He watched the men load their cannons, close the breech, and then step back a few paces behind the cannons with their hands clenched away from their sides.

"Why are they doing that?" asked the general. No one knew. After a lengthy investigation, he found an elderly English brigadier who explained to him, "Why they're simply 'olding their 'orses."

Holding their horses? Of course! In the past, the artillery had horse-drawn cannons. Back then, when the cannon was loaded but just before it was fired, the artillery men took a few paces backwards to hold the reins of the horses and keep them from running away. The horses had since been replaced by trucks, but the artillery men continued "to 'old the 'orses."

Genuine Leaders don't perpetuate meaningless procedures and tasks. They understand how silly and demoralizing these tasks can seem to the front-line associates of an organization.

If you don't like change, you'll like irrelevance even less.

Simon F. Cooper, CEO, Ritz-Carlton hotels

The history of a refund procedure at a brand-name retail outlet provides a good example of how a Genuine Leader discontinued an outmoded policy. The refund procedure stated that the customer had to go to the department in which he/she bought the item and try to resolve the complaint with the department manager. If the manager approved the complaint, the customer then had to go to the customer service desk to receive the refund. This certainly wasn't a consumer-friendly procedure.

A new store manager recognized the failings of this policy and immediately discontinued the counterproductive first step. The manager knew that approximately 18% of the customers who stop shopping at a particular store do so because of a bad refund experience. The simplified procedure was well received by the store's patrons.

Genuine Leaders analyze and discontinue procedures that should have never been introduced, that need an overhaul, or that have outlived their usefulness. They can pull the plug on a bad policy and move forward.

4. Discontinuing People

As stated in the introduction, you can categorize all of the people within an organization into four groups: Leaders, Managers, Participants, and Detractors. And while leaders, managers, and participants all contribute to the sum total of the organization's efforts, detractors take something away, such as energy, productivity, and morale. Genuine Leaders discontinue detractors by using that organization's approved discipline procedure.

Leaders often talk about getting the right people on the bus and throwing the wrong people off the bus. However, some leaders seem to think that they're on a plane, not a bus, and they're afraid to throw someone off because of the obvious consequences. Instead, they continue with all their detractors on board.

Stop trying to put out the fires. Instead, find the S.O.B. with the matches and put him or her out.

Michael DeFabis, Retired Executive and Mentor

The fear of firing someone must be one of the most widespread phobias among leaders. The thought of terminating someone makes many managers cringe and back away. But the odds against finding and hiring the right person every time for every position are impossibly high. When we occasionally hire the wrong person, we must correct the mistake and move on. Ignoring or transferring a problem associate can be extremely detrimental to an organization.

Bill was the most talented cook we ever employed but he had a very checkered personal life. Prior to joining us, he had serious challenges with drugs and alcohol. In the interview process, he assured us that he had been "clean" for five years and that he needed someone to believe in him. His passion for cooking, his maturity, and his candor earned him a spot on our team.

Four months into his job, Bill regrettably committed his second "No call, no show" offense, for which the punishment was termination. When I asked Bill's manager to process his termination papers, she responded, "But we can't fire Bill. He's the best cook we have." I replied, "But how can he be trusted to show up in the future? And what about the precedent we'd set if we ignored Bill's infractions?" In the end, Bill was released and replaced with someone almost as qualified and much more reliable.

Even if it hurts in the short run, Genuine Leaders have to make the tough calls. On the day we fired Bill, my manager began to be a better leader. She learned that the irreplaceable can be replaced and the indispensable can be dispensed with. Genuine Leaders know that they must do what's best for the organization in the long run.

While working for General Electric, Jack Welch annually fired 10% of his associates, those with the lowest performance evaluations. Welch said that he spent 75% of his time at GE evaluating associates and giving them honest assessments of their work. According to Welch, "It's cruel to keep your worst and then cut them when the tough times hit, after they've aged, have families, and have fewer choices." The success of GE speaks for itself. By looking at the numbers, Welch knew when to discontinue certain associates for the benefit of the business and, in most cases, for the benefit of the associate as well.

When evaluating an organization's termination process, there are three major considerations. First, is it legal and non-discriminatory? Second, is it fair and humane to the person being terminated? Third, is it administratively friendly; in other words, is the process simple, logical, and palatable for the person responsible for terminating the associate? If these criteria are not met, every effort should be made to correct the process. Otherwise, it will be avoided, circumvented, or totally ignored.

The 5-Step Discipline Process

Some managers find disciplining associates a daunting task, and they avoid doing it whenever they can. Managers seem to be afraid of losing a popularity contest. However, your staff, like your children, need enforced limits. When a rule infraction happens, you must deal with it swiftly and fairly. Rational and impartial discipline is a sign that you're paying attention to your associates and that you care about their performance.

Infractions fall into three categories: Not Serious, Mildly Serious, and Terminable. The 5-Step Discipline Process is best used for the "not serious" infractions, which form the majority of problems. These issues might include not greeting a customer, forgetting a name badge, being late for a shift, leaving a mess in the lunch room, etc. "Not serious" infractions shouldn't be overlooked; otherwise, they will morph into more serious issues.

If the infraction is "mildly serious" (for example, rudeness, breaking equipment, or profanity), you might want to start at Step 3 of the discipline process. Obviously, "terminable" infractions (such as stealing, abusive behavior, or substance abuse) require an immediate Step 5.

The 5-Step Discipline Process that I've used throughout my career works in both union and non-union shops. It's a positive system that is both user- and associate-friendly. Let's use a hypothetical associate named Michael to illustrate how the process works.

Step 1 – The Informal Talk

Michael, who's been working in your company for eight months, comes in late for the first time. You immediately call him aside to have a talk. You should hold this conversation in the workplace, not in your office, because this isn't a formal disciplinary session. You're not going to do a write-up. This is simply a discussion of the infraction between two adults.

First, you ask Michael if he knew that he was going to be late and why didn't he follow the procedures outlined in the associate handbook. Your conversation might sound something like this.

> *Manager:* "You might want to look at page 20 in the handbook, Michael. It specifically says that we expect you to call if you're going to be late."
>
> *Michael:* "I got a late start because my alarm clock didn't ring and the traffic was terrible."
>
> *Manager:* "Michael, I'm sure you have a cell phone or could get to a telephone to give us a call. Do you know why we ask you to call and let us know that you'll be late?"
>
> *Michael:* "I suppose you might have to call in a backup person if you think I'm not coming in."
>
> *Manager:* "Exactly. I've already called in Sam to work for you. Luckily, I happen to have enough work for both of you, but it's going to impact our payroll. All we needed was a quick phone call an hour before your start time, just as it says in the handbook. I hope you understand and that this won't happen again."

Stay upbeat and positive. This conversation is just a friendly reminder of what the rules are. But you must remember that any infraction of the company's rules must be dealt with, no matter how minor. The first step is vital to the disciplinary process. If you skip it, the associate will keep bending or breaking the rules. That's just human nature. And suddenly enforcing the rules after Michael is late five or six more times is not a good idea either. Should you suddenly decide to play hard ball, Michael would have the support of any arbitration panel.

Although Step 1 is a verbal action, make note of the date you had your conversation with Michael for your own personal records. You may eventually need to refer to this first action at some point in the future.

Step 2 – The Formal Talk

Two months later, Michael comes in late again. If it had been six months or more since the last infraction, then you would be justified in simply repeating Step 1. However, after only two months, it's time to move to Step 2, which means you call Michael into your office for a second conversation.

> *Manager:* "Michael, maybe you didn't think I was serious the last time we talked. Do you understand what the handbook says about being late?"

Your demeanor is pleasant, but by holding the meeting in your office, you've made it clear that this is a more serious conversation. You're demonstrating that you're serious about taking control of the situation.

Step 3 – First Written Notice

Three months later, Michael has come in late again without calling. This time, the meeting takes place in your office, with another manager or the union steward present. Be sure that at least one of the people in the room is the same gender as the associate so that there's less of a chance of the associate filing a harassment claim. Again, your conversation is about the infraction and what measures will be taken to correct the situation. In this meeting, you give Michael a formal, written memo that will be the first official company document in the process thus far. Below is an example of a typical Step 3 Memo.

> *Memo to: (Employee)*   *From: (Store Manager)*
> *Re: (Company Policy Infraction)*   *Date: (Meeting Date)*
> Today I talked to (associate) about (infraction). This is the third time (he/she) has violated company policy. We have already discussed the earlier infractions on (fill in dates of Step 1 and Step 2). (Associate) has indicated (he/she) will not do this again and will improve (his/her) job performance. (He/she) understands why we have the policy and how we administer it. I said that I had confidence that (he/she) could improve, and I advised (him/her) that if company policy were broken again, it would result in a one-day suspension.

You and the associate should both sign the memo, which is then placed in his/her file. End the meeting by reiterating that you have faith in the person's ability to get back on track and to follow the company's policies more diligently.

Step 4 – Second Written Notice

When Michael next comes in late or breaks any other rule, call him into your office again. Another manager or the union steward should be in attendance. This time, you must be sterner and make it clear that his job is on the line.

> *Manager:* "Michael, I've had to write you up for a second time. This is the fourth time we've talked about company policy infractions. Now, I'd like you to go home and think about whether you can – or will – follow our company policies. You've promised us three times that this wouldn't happen again, yet here we are. I'm disappointed in your behavior, so I'm suspending you for the remainder of the day. Tomorrow, please bring me a written plan of action that will show me how you intend to change your behavior."

Hopefully, Michael will show up on time the next morning with a plan for ensuring his prompt arrival at work. Michael's reaction to this exercise will give you a clear indication of his intentions. A thoughtful essay will show you that he's serious about wanting to stay. However, non-compliance or a cryptic sentence or two will not bode well for his future.

When you suspend an associate, you are taking definitive action that demonstrates you are dealing seriously with this repeated infraction of the rules. You want to give the person a wake-up call, so that he or she will think through the repercussions of his or her actions.

Step 5 – Termination

Michael has been late again, and this will be the third time that you've given him a write-up. This session will also be held in your office with a third party present. You should keep it short and to the point.

> *Manager:* "Michael, I'm sorry, we can't find a way to resolve the issue of your tardiness. It seems that all our efforts to help you have failed. Therefore, we are terminating our employment relationship, effective immediately. Your final paycheck will be ready on Friday at 3:00 p.m. I would appreciate it if you would please sign this final write-up detailing this discussion."

It's only natural to feel uneasy about taking this last step, but with the 5-Step Discipline Process, the associate will be able to accept your actions more easily. In fact, ever since adopting this 5-Step process, I have never had an associate lose his or her temper over his or her termination. Instead, he or she always seemed prepared for and resigned to what was coming.

The Pretenders will typically claim, "If I told them once, I told them a dozen times." But constantly repeating verbal warnings to your associates won't do the trick. Without a progressive next step, the violators will simply ignore you. And that's your fault, not theirs. When you utilize this 5-Step Progressive Discipline Process they'll get the message sooner. And you may be able to nip the problem in the bud during the first few steps, thus eliminating the need for future, more serious disciplinary interactions. Genuine Leaders know that the 5-Step Discipline Process shows firmness and fairness while being efficient and effective. Part of the power of this system is its simplicity.

The chart below summarizes the process.

THE PROGRESSIVE 5-STEP DISCIPLINE PROCESS

Step	Action	Location	Result
1	Verbal	Workplace	Swift action on first infraction
2	Verbal	Office	More serious second step
3	Written	Office	First Written documentation
4	Written	Office	Second Write-up and One-Day Suspension
5	Written	Office	Third Write-up and Termination

This progressive process is methodical, fair, and produces results. Leaders who commit to it find themselves in fewer arguments and unfair labor charges. In fact, after adopting this process myself, I was less reluctant to initiate a disciplinary action because of the non-confrontational verbal, not written, first two steps. Then, if problem employee continued their poor behavior all the way to Step 5, I never felt it was mismanagement that caused their termination.

Most employees say that they welcome fair and consistent discipline from their supervisors. Of the thousands of associates I've surveyed over the years, 60 percent say their company is not aggressive enough in dealing with poor performers. I've asked dozens and dozens of audiences to think of their all-time favorite teacher. Then, I bet them that same teacher was one of the toughest, strictest teachers they ever had. Interestingly, an overwhelming majority of the people readily agree. You see, most of us don't respect the Pretenders who ignore our mistakes or hand us unearned A's or easy ways out of a bad situation. Rather, we respect the Genuine Leaders who hold us accountable and challenge us to stretch ourselves beyond our self-imposed limitations.

If you discontinue bad before worse happens... that will be good.

Genuine Leader

Genuine Leaders Make the Tough Calls

In his book *Leadership,* former New York City mayor Rudolph Giuliani recounts the story of President Reagan and the air traffic controllers. In August 1981, Giuliani was the associate Attorney General; as such, he was privy to exactly what happened during the clash between the controller's union (PATCO) and the U.S. government. After several months of threats, three-quarters of the union's 17,000 membership walked off the job, paralyzing airline travel and precipitating a long meeting with the Justice Department and the President.

Giuliani remembers that, as the meeting was breaking up, President Reagan asked, "Didn't they take an oath?" Reagan knew what everyone else had overlooked, forgotten, or not realized. Every government employee signs an oath swearing that they will never go on strike against the United States. The Justice Department had to look up the employment forms to verify that the president was indeed correct. Every striking controller had signed a form that said:

> *I am not participating in any strike against the Government of the United States or any agency thereof, and I will not so participate while an employee of the Government of the United States or any agency thereof.*

The strike was therefore illegal. The President held steadfast and enforced the law, firing all those who didn't return to work within 48 hours. The union was sure that the President was bluffing, but they found out that he wasn't when he "discontinued" 11,000 detractors – union members who were breaking the law.

SUMMARY SCORE:

How good are you at discontinuing procedures, equipment, processes, or associates that have outlived their usefulness and are in need of replacement? Are you a decisive leader who isn't afraid to change the status quo when you can to improve the operation, procedure, process, or personnel? Or would you rather stand back and wait to see if things improve by themselves, thus sparing you the necessity of taking charge?

Score yourself using a 1-10 scale

Recommendations to Raise Your *Ability to Discontinue Things* Score:

1. Don't let it die; kill it first.

Make this phrase one of your top mantras. Genuine Leaders rapidly learn to embrace the art of letting go. Attempting to coddle a dying endeavor or a futile policy is insane.

2. Have a post-project debriefing.

A month after we opened our first restaurant, I held a post-project debriefing with the contractor, the project manager and my management team. The purpose was to identify construction practices that we should repeat in our next store as well as to identify any procedures that were too costly or time consuming. The process was extremely productive. Through this meeting, we eliminated thousands of dollars of costs from future projects.

Within a month of a project's completion, have a meeting with your team to review the experience. Build your discussion around these four questions:

- What did we do well?
- What did we do poorly?
- What did we learn from this?
- How can we do better the next time?

3. To keep or not to keep?

To decide if a policy or procedure should be discontinued in your organization, review why it was started in the first place, and then determine if that reason is still applicable today. If not, discontinue it. For example, many company picnics were permanently canceled because of lawsuits that arose from accidents caused by alcohol that had been consumed during the events. Organizations could think of no other alternative but to discontinue company picnics and holiday parties. I felt those leaders who discontinued their company picnics were misguided and uncreative.

We determined that our company picnic was originally intended as a fun time for our employees and their families. Company functions provide an enormous morale boost. Instead of discontinuing our company functions, we decided to discontinue alcohol abuse at company functions.

4. What's stupid around here?

Conduct a "What's Stupid Around Here?" essay contest for your associates. Post the winners on your bulletin board or in your newsletter. Offer prizes for the ideas that are the "most stupid," "most counter-productive," or "most customer-unfriendly." You're sure to identify policies and procedures that you'll want to discontinue. But keep in mind that when you solicit your associates' ideas on what is "stupid," you must be prepared to change or discontinue the practices.

5. "Work-as-a-Clerk."

One of my clients, a senior manager, was particularly committed to my "Work-as-a-Clerk" program. Each month he "worked" the life of an associate for four continuous hours. In doing so, he discovered the "Triple 7" discipline policy that had been created right under his nose but which he knew nothing about. The "Triple 7" meant that if you as a store manager failed to make your budget for two weeks in a row, you would be forced into a work schedule of 7 a.m. to 7 p.m., 7 days a week (Triple 7) until you met your budget.

This punishment had been created by a network of supervising middle managers, but wasn't sanctioned by top management. My client felt embarrassingly out of touch for not knowing about this practice. His "Work-as-a-Clerk" assignment helped him to finally understand his high turnover rate among store managers. Threats and additional hours don't motivate, they alienate. He quickly abolished the practice of Triple 7, along with those who created it.

The closer you are to the operations, the more obvious it will become that

velop Others for Good Reasons

enuine Leaders produce more than their fair share of
ple in their organizations. Pretenders, on the other hand,
their people.

d that:

evelop may ultimately threaten my position, so it's better
where they are."

ve to do more work when the associate gets promoted."
I need is to go through the process of finding a
vacated position."

unter with:

e of my team reflects my leadership skills, so it's
p the team members develop their potentials. I can't
g in the organization if I don't have able people ready

op our people, the talented, ambitious ones will leave
re fulfilling experience elsewhere. Inevitably, we will
and we will have lost valuable assets."

level of performance in my area by developing and
e, I'll have more qualified people to whom I can
workload, and I'll be able to spend more time on my

> turning point this season
> hen our players began to believe
> re about them personally
>   than I do about winning.
>
> *Avery Johnson, Coach, National Basketball Association*

velop Others

g with Emotional Intelligence, author Daniel
ask of leadership is emotional. People don't leave
they go out the door. We have feelings all the
tune in to those feelings and move them in a

you'll need to discontinue some things. Genuine Leaders do need to "work as
a clerk." They're humbled by what they learn in the process and are prepared
to discontinue inappropriate policies, procedures, and people.

6. Discontinue things wholeheartedly.

Misguided managers often deal with problem associates by transferring
them to another department within the same company. Genuine Leaders tackle
the problem directly. They don't pass it off to someone else.

7. Keep problem employees on a manager's to-do list.

Terminating an associate should be the last resort. As we discussed, there
are four steps that you can take to adjust an associate's behavior and
performance before you fire him or her. Therefore, make sure the name of any
under-performer is on a manager's weekly planner until that associate has
either developed into an acceptable performer who is an asset to the
organization or is deemed "unsalvageable" and is subsequently terminated.

RECOMMENDED READING
- **The Leadership Challenge**
  by James M. Kouzes and Barry Z. Posner *(Jossey-Bass, 1995)*
- **Jack Welch on Leadership**
  by Robert Slater *(McGraw-Hill, 2004)*
- **Leadership**
  by Rudolph W. Giuliani and Ken Kurson *(Miramax, 2002)*

GE

DE

As iron

so

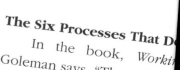

Genuine Leaders De

It's a fact that G

promotion-worthy peo

are reluctant to develo

Pretenders conten

- "The people I d

to keep them right

- "I'll probably ha

- "The last thing

replacement for the

Genuine Leaders co

- "The performan

important that I he

improve my standin

to take my place."

- "If we don't devel

us to search for a m

have vacancies to fil

- "If I bring up the

promoting my peop

delegate some of my

own goals."

Our team's

was w

that I care mo

The Six Processes That D

In the book, *Worki*

Goleman says, "The primal

their feelings at home whe

time, and the best leaders

positive direction."

Employees are like spouses: if they're not shown attention and appreciation, they'll go somewhere else. Members of your organization need to feel accepted and to experience achievement. Your associates' needs can be summarized by the following "A-List":

Acceptance. We all need to belong.

Attention. We all need to be noticed.

Appreciation. We all need to feel valued.

Achievement. We all need success and meaningful accomplishments.

The six processes that will help you develop your people are Orientation, Communication, Discipline, Recognition, Performance Updates, and the Written Exit Interview. They may be familiar, but most leaders fail to use them well. We've talked about the Communication and Discipline processes in earlier chapters. Now, we'll concentrate on the remaining four.

Process 1: Orientation

Genuine Leaders know that their real work begins the minute employment is offered to an individual. And the four questions every new associate wants answered ASAP are:

- What's my job?
- How will my performance be measured?
- Who will measure it?
- Where will I go from here?

An effective Orientation Process will address all four questions during the associate's first 30 days. Notice that we use the term "orientation" instead of the often-used "probationary period." While one definition of probation is "subjection of an individual to a period of testing and trial to ascertain fitness as for a job or school," the most common connotation is that of criminals trying to prove their acceptance back into society. We shouldn't use a term with such negative implications when we're trying to welcome a new associate. Isn't it better to be positive? We should say, "Welcome to the company. For the next month you'll participate in an Orientation Process to help you adapt to your new job and feel comfortable working with us."

A basic Orientation Process for entry level associates should include these eight events:

• **A warm, celebratory welcome** the moment the new associate arrives on Day One. Be prepared for the associate's arrival, and show your pleasure that he or she has joined your team.

- **A short bio and a picture** of the associate should be posted on the company's bulletin board. Take the picture during the final interview when you offer the job.
- A "**New Employee Kit**" to be reviewed with the new associate during the first hour on the job. The kit should include the 12 items below:

NEW EMPLOYEE KIT
1. Welcome Checklist that includes Management's Top 10 expectations and promises
2. Employee Handbook
3. Organization's Mission Statement
4. Job Description (for the new associate's specific position)
5. Sample Assignment Sheet (To-Do List)
6. Various Legal Forms (e.g., I-9 forms)
7. Emergency Phone Numbers
8. Work Schedule Card (showing the first two weeks in advance)
9. Performance Review Form
10. 5-Step Discipline Process Outline
11. Name Badge (if applicable, with first name and last initial)
12. Glossary of Industry-Related Terms

- **A 30-minute tour** of the workplace with introductions to as many associates as time permits.
- A "**debriefing**" **session** scheduled for the last 10 minutes of the first day. Never let a new associate leave the job on Day One without spending a few minutes reviewing the first day with him or her.
- **A brief phone call from the leader to the associate's home** two weeks into the relationship to discuss his or her feelings about the job. This call, which should be made between 7:00 p.m. and 9:00 p.m., shows personal interest, indirectly involves the associate's family, and can be conducted without on-the-job interference. I've used this practice often, and I've had great results.
- **A meeting after 30 days** to review the associate's progress, officially making the transition from being a new hire to being one of the family.
- **The scheduling of the associate's first formal performance review**, which could take place after six months and up to a year. Scheduling this important date gives the associate something meaningful to look forward to.

A Very Bad Beginning

Ever since she was three years old, my daughter Randee has been fascinated with cash registers. Her favorite toy was a little plastic cash register. I never remember Randee with a doll, but I do remember her cash register. So it came as no surprise to me that as soon as she turned 16, she wanted to work as a supermarket cashier.

Her job interview was set for 2:00 p.m., and her mother drove her to the big event. Randee was all dressed up, and we'd thoroughly coached her on the questions that she was most likely to be asked. She even had her entire summer schedule typed up, showing the eight or nine days she needed for family events so that her boss would be forewarned and could plan accordingly.

I could hardly wait to hear what happened during the interview. Unfortunately, Randee's disappointment broke my heart. She got the job, but the way she got it frustrated her immensely. Apparently, Randee looked so qualified and was so prepared that the interviewer hired her on the spot. He asked Randee only two questions: "Are you 16 or older?" and "When can you start?"

Some might think that Randee should be happy because she was hired so quickly, but she didn't see it like that. She felt they acted in haste or in desperation. And the first two days of her orientation were nightmares. In fact, she cried herself to sleep both nights. During Randee's first two days, the following occurred:

• She was given a nametag with someone else's name on it because the store didn't have a blank nametag and the label maker was broken. Her superior told her, "We know it's not your name, but management insists you wear a nametag." For over a week, people referred to her as "Brittany," the name on the temporary tag.

• She was issued a soiled uniform that reeked of cigarettes and was missing the middle button. The uniform was a cashier's smock, but she wasn't trained as a cashier. For two weeks, various managers, upon seeing her cashier smock, would order her to open a certain register. When she told one manager she couldn't because she didn't know how to, he barked, "What can you do?"

• On her first night, five minutes before her scheduled departure time, the manager in charge told Randee to clean the restrooms, which is at least a 30-minute task. She had never been shown where the mop and bucket were located or how to do the job, and nobody had told her that she'd have to leave work 25 minutes late on her first night.

- Astoundingly, Randee was never introduced to any of the store managers for over a week.

Randee barely lasted the summer, and she'll never work in a supermarket again. Who can blame her? Not surprisingly, six of the seven people hired on the same day as Randee quit within a week. An effective Orientation Process could have eliminated most of this turnover. Fully 80% of all terminations that occur in an associate's first 30 days are the fault of management, not the employee!

A Friend to Lean On

A very practical and effective method in developing a new recruit is to have him or her follow a model employee. Utilizing the most qualified associate to orient a new candidate makes sense. This process is referred to as "shadowing" when it involves the orientation of a new associate and "mentoring" when it involves a management candidate.

Depending on the position and the frequency of interactions, shadowing/mentoring relationships can last for any length of time, from 30 days to over a year. Unlike training manuals and computer-based instruction, shadowing/mentoring takes place in the working environment. Learning takes place in the actual job site, not in a training cubicle. The instructors are regular employees, people who know and perform the job well. Real life situations are used to build an understanding of how the organization works. Learning relies on conversation and observation, not just on lectures. For many newcomers, the shadowing/mentoring process greatly helps to demystify the magnitude of the job.

One of the many side benefits of the shadowing/mentoring process is that the new associate often builds a lasting relationship with his/her assigned leader. Although the transfer of technical skills is the primary goal of the process, its social benefits are just as valuable. Another benefit of the shadowing/mentoring process is that the new associate can observe the intricacies of the entire organization and understand how the parts interact as a whole.

When you select an organization's mentors, you must be extremely careful. A poor mentor could sour a candidate who has loads of potential. Former General Electric CEO Jack Welch has said, "Pairing up an employee with a single mentor is one of the stupidest ideas around in management because the mentor may be a turkey." However, I'd argue that instead of axing the entire mentoring process, you should be very thorough in selecting your mentors, and you should rotate the new associate between two or more mentors. If you construct a quick T-Bar Analysis of the mentoring process, you'll find a far greater point total on the left (the pluses) than on the right (the minuses).

T-Bar Analysis of the Mentoring Process

(+)	(-)
Quicker indoctrination of associate...7	Opportunity cost of occupying another associate to mentor the new associate...6
More control over what is taught to the new associate. 9	You've chosen a mentor who does a poor job, causing the new associate to leave. 3
More rapid social interaction 4	
Less employee turnover. 10	
Mentors develop leadership skills in the process. 3	
Total 33	Total 9

When positive instructional feedback closely follows real-time experience, learning will grow exponentially. My company gave mentors additional compensation, and we considered their role and responsibilities to be important steps in their own development process as well as in those of new associates.

The benefits of mentoring have been shown throughout history. As Ralph Waldo Emerson wrote, "There is no teaching until the pupil is brought into the same state or principle in which you are; a transformation takes place, he is you and you are he; there is a teaching and by no unfriendly chance or bad company can he ever quite lose the benefit."

A thorough and sincere orientation program builds a foundation of trust between management and associates. The program is defined by the activities used to carefully acclimate a new associate to the organization. Too often, all that separates the "welcome" and the "get to work" is a heartbeat. Instead, there should be 20 to 40 hours of activities spread over the first 30 days.

Good Question:	"What if I commit the time and money to really orient/train my new associates and they quit?"
Better Question:	"But, what if you don't and they stay?"

The Vicious Cycle of an Inadequate Orientation/Training Process

An orientation program shouldn't be considered a luxury or an option. The cost of orientation is an important investment – maybe the most important investment you can make. Here's an example that illustrates what I mean.

1. Your dishwasher (fill in any hourly position) quits due to the frustration from inadequate orientation/training, **and SO**...

2. Other associates must cover for the departed dishwasher by ignoring part of their jobs, resulting in less-than-desirable customer service, **and SO**...

3. The manager on duty is forced to spend more time with customers' complaints due to less attentive service, **and SO**...

4. The manager can't spend sufficient time training associates because of the time spent dealing with complaints, **and SO**...

5. Complaints ultimately result in lost business, which causes a cutback in expenses. Consequently, labor hours and training time get further reduced, **and SO**...

6. Another employee quits because of the frustration caused by inadequate orientation/training **and SO**...the vicious, downward spiral continues.

Ben Franklin once wrote, "For the want of a nail, the shoe was lost; for the want of a shoe the horse was lost; and for the want of a horse the rider was lost, being overtaken and slain by the enemy, all for the want of a horseshoe nail." I contend that for the want of an effective orientation program, many employees will be lost.

Process 2: Communication

In Chapter Three, we addressed communication: listening, speaking, and writing. We also discussed many systems used to foster communication in an organization, including:

• Memos paper-clipped to paychecks
• Bulletin boards
• Monthly T.E.A.M. meetings
• "What's Stupid Around Here?" sessions
• Open door policies
• Daily "huddle-ups"

The ideas in Chapter Three demonstrate how your communication skills play an essential part in the development process of your associates. You might take a moment to review them before proceeding.

Process 3: Discipline/Correcting Problem Behaviors

Medical columnist Dr. Peter Gott wrote, "Discipline is guidance, not punishment." I learned that lesson well in high school.

Mrs. Helen Van Eseltine, my French teacher, was a strict disciplinarian who was intensely passionate about developing her students. She doled out many rigorous homework assignments, but she never seemed fazed by the workload she created for herself. Mrs. Van Eseltine's three or more quizzes per week were legendary. Who could forget the dreaded words, "Fermez vos livres et prenez une feuille de papier (Close your books and take out a piece of paper)?" I never will. Why did I elect to take French from seventh grade through senior year, when only two years were required? Simple. Mrs. Van Eseltine.

None of my other teachers ever came close to duplicating Mrs. Van Eseltine's passion for teaching. She was the epitome of a Genuine Leader in the classroom, and she had an unparalleled desire to bring out the potential in each and every student.

I'm deeply grateful to Mrs. Van Eseltine. Her disciplined approach to teaching allowed me to develop from an average student to an accomplished one. She was the leader I so desperately needed at that time in my life. If you become a "Mrs. Van Eseltine" for your associates, they'll never forget what you did for them, and they'll always be grateful.

Process 4: Recognition

There are two things people want more than sex and money... recognition and praise.

Mary Kay Ash, founder, Mary Kay Cosmetics

Genuine Leaders are comfortable with letting their associates know how much they are appreciated. They can demonstrate this gratitude in a variety of ways, including a remodeled break room, an awards banquet, a birthday card mailed to the associate's home, a certification pin and plaque after completing an advanced skills training, or a note of thanks attached to a paycheck.

My organization's Self-Development Fund was a unique recognition program that my managers greatly appreciated. I would budget $500 per year for each manager to use to develop their professional skills or personal well-being. Some used it to continue their education. Others used it to buy a piece of gym equipment or to join a health club. One associate even used the money to pay for hypnosis in an attempt to quit smoking.

The Self-Development Fund was successful for two reasons. First, those who used it as intended became better individuals in some way, to increase their "personal asset value." Second, those who didn't take advantage of the program inadvertently gave a loud and clear signal of their true ambitions with the company. The managers had only two requirements to fulfill in order to receive $500 each year. The first was to have been a manager for at least a year, and the second was an essay explaining how they intended to spend the money.

Incredibly, there were always a few managers who passed on the $500 offer. If Genuine Leaders are continuously self-developing, what does it say about those Pretenders who couldn't figure out how to spend $500 to better themselves? The program taught me who were potential leaders and who talked a lot about wanting to become a leader but didn't have what former Chrysler leader Lee Iacocca calls "a fire in the belly."

Recognition for your associates should be progressive. As an associate continues to perform at higher and higher levels, his or her recognition should grow proportionally. For example, you might begin with a few pats on the back, then move up to a letter of commendation placed in his or her file, then an acknowledgement of his or her achievement in the company newsletter, and finally a pay raise and a promotion. Simply saying "Way to go!" over and over will sound hollow over time, just as a dozen verbal warnings will lose their effectiveness.

Process 5: The Performance Review

What gets measured gets done.
What gets measured and recognized gets done even better.

Author Unknown

If you've done your job as a leader, your associates should know your organization's mission statement – preferably by heart, but at least in principle. Since almost everyone has a personal mission or personal objectives, Genuine Leaders take the time to learn them and try to demonstrate where the organization and the individual share common objectives. This allows them to achieve what I call the Relational Overlap, which is shown here in the shaded area.

Relational Overlap

An example of the shaded area (shared objective) might be a cross-training program, in which the company develops a more versatile associate and the associate acquires additional industry-related skills.

Shared objectives tend to open lines of communication and build stronger intra-company relationships. How has your organization aligned itself to the needs and wants of your associates? The best forum to discover where shared objectives may exist is the associate's performance review.

Conducting a performance review for every associate is the most important long-term leadership responsibility. It is the single most effective way to develop associates and discover their personal objectives.

Not surprisingly, great organizations are committed to a comprehensive performance review process, but below-average companies are not. In fact, many sub-standard companies report that they skip performance reviews because "most of our employees aren't around long enough to get an annual review." How's that for a self-fulfilling prophecy?

It's difficult to understand why some leaders are not committed to performance reviews. Although most leaders like to boast that their associates are their greatest assets, many seem reluctant to spend the time and intellectual energy it takes to help these assets appreciate in value through a performance review process. I've concluded that too many leaders are unsure how to conduct a review and are thus uneasy doing them. If this explanation rings a bell with you, read on.

After conducting almost four hundred performance reviews, I identified Ten Important Practices (TIPs) you can use in associate performance reviews. I wasn't given this advice in college, graduate school, or in an entry-level management job. I had to figure out these TIPs the hard way, through my own trial and error.

As you begin to review these TIPs, slow your reading speed down by one-third. Absorb each word and sentence. All of the ideas are important and non-negotiable. I've taught them for over 20 years, and they work for any and every organization that is committed to developing its people.

10 TIPS to a More Effective Performance Review Process

1. Offer One Week's Notice

Offer the associate at least one week's notice before the review so he/she can prepare his or her thoughts, ideas, and goals. Give the associate a blank performance review form to complete about themselves, and ask him/her to submit that form to you a day or two prior to the actual review. This will allow you to see how the associate evaluates his/her performance, and it will allow you to identify areas that may require additional thought and preparation.

If you find that your associate's rating and your rating are off by 20% or more (for example, your score was a 4 and his or her score was a 6 on a 1-10 scale), be sure to clearly identify examples to support your score – or be prepared to change it.

2. Be Mindful of the 50/50 Preparation/Presentation Guideline

Spend as much time preparing for the review as you spend conducting it. A 60-minute performance review will require 60 minutes of prep time to do the job correctly. Your thorough preparation will set the stage for a productive review. During the preparation time, you should review the associate's self-review, talk to previous supervisors, review his or her current job description, look through the associate's file, and begin to create goals for the associate's next 12 months.

3. Arrange for Privacy, Comfort, and Sufficient Time

Ask your assistant to hold all calls during the review. Make this request in front of the associate so that he/she sees how much importance you attach to the process. I can't stress this enough. There can be no interruptions!

Reviewing a "prime-time" (part-time) associate requires a minimum of 30 minutes. A full-time employee requires a full hour. Plan on 90 minutes for a middle manager, and take two hours with your top management.

Never look at your watch during the review process. Take it off and leave it in your desk drawer. By looking at your watch, you might make your associates feel like you have something more important on your mind.

4. "Two-on-One" Reviews

The performance review process is a vital growth strategy for both the associate and the company. To maximize the process's positive impact, the meeting should include at least three people: the associate, the reviewer, and the reviewer's immediate boss. With the reviewer's boss in attendance, the reviewer is more likely to be more thorough and objective. You'll find that this two-on-one arrangement benefits all parties involved. The associate gets to shine in front of two upper levels of management. The reviewer can demonstrate to the boss how well he or she develops his or her people over time. And during the review, the big boss can conduct an informal personnel inventory to identify future stars or areas in need of improvement.

Be mindful of the seating arrangement – you don't want your associate to feel intimated with a "two-against-one" setup. In the associate's first review, the reviewer should sit on one side of a rectangular table, facing the associate and the reviewer's boss on the other side. Having the boss's boss on the associate's side tends to bolster the associate's confidence. In subsequent years, the seating arrangement won't matter as much because most of the associate's fear and misconceptions about the process will have dissipated once they realize all parties in attendance want the same thing: the associate's positive development.

5. The "70-25-5" Rule

Here is a guideline for how much each of the three people present should talk during the review:

- The associate should command 70% of the conversation.
- The primary reviewer should talk about 25% of the time.
- The senior manager or big boss is restricted to 5 % of the discussion, occasionally interjecting some insightful comments or questions.

This 70%-25%-5% ratio is difficult to achieve during the first performance review because the associate will likely be nervous and apprehensive about the process. As the associate realizes that all parties present are only there to help develop his/her potential, he or she will begin to relax and will consequently talk more. If you maintain this 70%-25%-5% ratio, the reviewer will be forced to listen more, thereby gaining greater understanding.

6. Show that You Listen and You Can Be Flexible

Use two pens with different colored inks during the review process. The reviewer will have completed the evaluation form in one color, e.g., black. The second color, perhaps blue or green, should be used to make changes, additions, and deletions on the appraisal form during the review itself. If the associate makes a reasonable argument regarding a score or comment, you might alter your review to agree with him/her. This note-taking visibly demonstrates that you listen, respect the other's viewpoint, and are willing to change.

7. Avoid the "Halo," "Sandwich," and "Recent-cy" Effects

The "Halo Effect" happens if a reviewer has a personal bias towards one performance category and therefore arbitrarily skews all of the other scores. For example, you might believe that customer service is the most important part of an associate's job. As a result, you'll give higher scores on all criteria to an associate who is really good with customers. However, it's important to measure each criterion separately, objectively, and independently from the others.

The "Sandwich Effect" occurs if you always position a critical remark between compliments. Many reviewers use "sandwiching" because they're afraid to confront an issue. For example, they might say, "Ellen, you're very personable with the guests, but your cash control is poor. But don't get me wrong. We're very grateful you're so loyal." This technique will only confuse your associates. Instead of trying to dodge a problem by sandwiching it with compliments, take time to discuss the issue directly and find ways to resolve it. Remember, you're not attacking the person, you're attacking the problem.

The "Recent-cy" Effect is far too common and is difficult to avoid. We tend to remember the most recent incidents and judge an annual performance on events that occurred last week or last month. You must consider the full performance period in a review, not just what has happened recently.

8. Complete the Entire Form

Fill all available space on the review form with comments, examples, elaborations, and clarifications. When you leave your present position, your reviews will remain behind for the next manager to reference. A score of B (on an A-to-F scale) or a 3 (on a 1-10 scale) mean nothing without detailed explanations. The managers who follow you need to know what you meant by your grade. Make sure that you clarify your assessments with some details and examples. Clear, specific, and honest comments and examples result in a better review process and build mutual trust. Also, your specificity will train you to observe and assess your associates more fairly and precisely, which benefits both them and the company.

9. Separate Performance Reviews and Pay Adjustments Discussions

Although pay and performance are almost always connected, you should wait at least a month after the performance review to discuss a pay adjustment.

I used to end the review process by announcing how much the associate's pay would be adjusted as a result of his or her previous year's performance. This was a huge mistake. In time, I realized that the associates weren't really listening to what was discussed until the issue of money was brought up. In the worse case scenario, which happened far too often, the associate received a smaller raise than he or she had anticipated. The associate's disappointment far outweighed any positive results that had been generated in the previous 60 minutes, thus effectively negating the value of the review process.

By creating some time space between these two discussions, the associates can digest their performance goals before they think about any pay adjustments.

10. End with a Positive Goal-Setting Session

Goal-setting should make up 70% of the review because this process will have the most positive impact on everyone involved. Specific goals give the associate a clear direction regarding what he/she must do to improve and grow with the company.

Write these goals carefully, and use the S.M.A.R.T. techniques that we've previously discussed. Goals should address the associate's strengths ("How can we best utilize this human asset in other parts of the company?") and should consider the associate's weaknesses ("What can we do to improve?").

Depending on their difficulty levels, the number of goals that an associate takes on should range from three to seven. For those associates with whom you've already developed a strong rapport, you might want to make one of their S.M.A.R.T. goals personal in nature. For example, ask them, "What one personal goal would you like to accomplish this year that I can help you achieve?" By asking this question, I've been instrumental in helping many associates stop smoking, go back to school, read more, and even improve their golf games. Their appreciation for my interest in their personal lives was sincere. Remember, the job of a leader is to take their people to levels that they couldn't reach by themselves.

Process 6: The Written Exit Interview

People are going to leave your company, either voluntarily or involuntarily. Whatever the reason for termination of employment, you must know why the separation occurred. Therefore, a well-executed exit interview process is vital to minimize employee turnover.

The exit interview is a written interaction between a manager and an associate that is primarily focused on the reasons why that associate is leaving the company. This interview can occur the moment the associate gives notice, on the associate's last day, or two to four weeks after the associate has left. It's easier to ensure that the interview will occur if the associate is still on site. However, a delayed interview may generate a higher quality of response because any highly-charged emotions will have had time to cool down.

Experience has taught me to use both methods. Using the first initial of the associate's last name, I would alternate the two different approaches. Names that begin with A, C, E, G, etc. would have interviews done before the departing associate leaves the premises for the last time. Last names beginning with B, D, F, H, etc. would receive an exit interview in the mail two to three weeks after leaving the company. While I receive a greater total number of interviews from those completed before the associates leave the job, the quality and detail of the delayed interviews usually seems to be higher.

Although some companies rely on a verbal exit interview, this method doesn't work as well for two main reasons. First, in many companies, the exit interviewer is typically the associate's immediate supervisor. The associate will often be reluctant to give honest feedback to the manager who may be a part of the reason the associate is leaving. Second, once the associate gives his or her reasons for leaving verbally, someone else must interpret them in order to write them down. Many comments, such as, "management doesn't listen to us," could be misconstrued and misrepresented, either intentionally or unintentionally.

To limit inaccurate interpretations and to achieve some consistency in the exit interview process, it's best to use a written form. At the end of this chapter, I've provided a template that you can adapt for your specific organization. You should strive for simplicity, comprehensiveness, and speed. Limit the form to 10 to 12 questions that will take about 10 minutes to complete.

One of the benefits of a written exit interview is that it remains in your files for later reference. For instance, if a higher-than-average associate turnover rate emerges in a particular division, a thorough review of all exit interviews from the last six months will often help identify the source of the problem. Remember "finding the tick" from Chapter Two? Here is another case where it is critical to find the real cause of the problem, not just the more obvious symptom that you see.

Genuine Leaders know that if they want to build a cohesive corporate culture, they need to slow the speed of employee turnover out the proverbial "revolving door." Through the use of written exit interviews, you'll discover clues as to what may be broken in your company, and you'll have a better chance of fixing your problems sooner rather than later.

Teaching Someone How to Fish

Give a man a fish
and you'll feed him for a day.
Teach a man how to fish
and he'll stop
showing up for work.

Pretender

One of my favorite sayings is, "Give a man a fish and you'll feed him for a day. Teach a man how to fish and you'll feed him for a lifetime." This Chinese proverb perfectly describes why we should develop our associates. A dear friend of mine, Pete Luckett, a three-time Canadian Independent Retailer of the Year, is a Genuine Leader who likes to say, "Exceptional customer experiences begin with passionate performers." Pete would be the first to agree that most passionate performers are developed over time as a result of lots of personal attention and skills training. Genuine Leaders are willing to make this investment for the long-term benefit of the organization.

In business, as well as in our personal lives, our ultimate *raison d'etre* is to carry out our mission, whatever it may be. Genuine Leaders know their chances of successfully achieving their objectives are significantly increased through the development of others along the way.

A manager multiplies his own knowledge and
skills when he imparts them to his subordinates.
When he can transfer the knowledge and skills
of other capable people to his employees,
he increases their value
by another order of magnitude.

Lester R. Bittel, management expert

SUMMARY SCORE:

How much time, energy, thought and passion do you dedicate to the development of your people?

Score yourself on a scale of 1-10

Recommendations to Raise Your *Develops Others* Score:

1. Identify which side of this Attitude Ledger best represents you.

Pretenders say...	Genuine Leaders say...
1. "Help Wanted"	1. "Now interviewing for..."
2. "They're just employees, a necessary evil."	2. "They're our associates, the key to our success."
3. "Training them is a huge expense."	3. "Training them is a lucrative investment."
4. "They are here for a paycheck nothing more, nothing less."	4. "Working here will be a life-long experience they'll remember forever."

2. Rate how your organization performs the Six Associate Development Processes on a scale of 1-to-20:

    a. Our Orientation Process is (out of 20)   ____

    b. Our Communication is (out of 20)   ____

    c. Our Discipline Process is (out of 20)   ____

    d. Our Recognition Programs are (out of 20)   ____

    e. Our Performance Reviews are (out of 20)   ____

    f. Our Exit Interviewing Process is ...(out of 10)   +____ Bonus

                                        Grand Total   ____

If your grand total score is less than 70, reprioritize your goals for the coming year to make the development of these six processes your top priority. This book gives you all the information you need to raise your score well above

80. Nothing great will ever result from an organization that fails to deliver at least a 60 on this simple diagnostic self-test.

3. Make certain each of your best managers has at least one person to mentor.

Keep a scorecard on his or her success as a mentor. Some managers are more gifted teachers than others. Utilize the most talented mentors more often and give them appropriate recognition for their added contribution to the organization.

4. Conduct "This Is What I Learned This Month" luncheons.

Ask all attendees to share the one thing they learned since the last session that has most favorably impacted their job performance and/or satisfaction. Keep a log of all submissions and refer to them periodically to check that the associates continue to use their new knowledge or skills.

5. Consider a Self-Development Fund for as many associates as you can afford.

Budget $100 to $500 a year per associate and invite them to invest in something that will grow their Personal Asset Value. This fund will go a long way toward fostering a culture of personal development within your organization.

6. Emphasize learning as a core value of your organization.

Make books, e-learning courses, and internal or external classes available for those who wish to grow. Encourage all associates to learn and to teach each and every day.

> ## If you have knowledge,
> ## let others light their candles with it.
> *Sir Winston Churchill, British statesman*

RECOMMENDED READING
➡ Performance Management: A Pocket Guide for Employee Development by James Rollo and Bob King *(Goal/QPC, 2001)*
➡ Leading at a Higher Level: Blanchard on Leadership and Creating High Performing Organizations by Ken Blanchard *(FT Press, 2006)*
➡ Make Their Day! Employee Recognition that Works by Cindy Ventrice *(Berrett-Koehler Publishers, 2003)*

Chapter Seven Appendix:

SAMPLE EMPLOYEE EXIT INTERVIEW

1. What led you to interview with us in the first place?_____
_____

2. Was the position offered to you properly described during
the hiring process? _____
_____

3. Did you receive adequate orientation/training to perform your job?
(Please explain)_____
_____   _____

4. Did you have a good working relationship with your Manager and/or
Department Manager? (Please explain) _____
_____

5. What impressed you least about our company? _____
_____

6. What impressed you most about our company?_____
_____

7. What did you like least about your job? _____
_____

8. What did you like most about your job? _____
_____

9. If your separation was voluntary, what could we have done to
lengthen your employment? _____
_____

10. If your separation was voluntary, may we place you on
our Seasonal/Temporary list of employees and call you back on
occasion if your schedule permits?   Yes _____No _____
If yes, your phone number please: _____

Name: (Optional)_____   Date: _____

GENUINE LEADERS ARE CONTINUOUSLY SELF-DEVELOPING

Whatever authority I may have rests solely on knowing how much I do not know.

Socrates, ancient Greek philopher

Growing Your Personal Asset Value

One of the most prudent long-term investments you can make for your company is an investment in your own personal development. It doesn't matter how old you are or what position you hold in the organization. And the sooner you begin the process, the more your Personal Asset Value (PAV) will increase. You bring your unique, personal knowledge and skill set to the organization or corporate "classroom." But if your PAV isn't updated and revitalized, like most assets, it will depreciate steadily over time. Genuine Leaders never stop learning. They know that success occurs at the intersection of preparation and opportunity.

Your PAV defines your economic worth to the organization. If you cease adding to your own PAV, your value to the organization decreases, especially in today's competitive business environment. Unless you increase your PAV by continuously developing your mental and physical capabilities, you're shortchanging not only yourself but also your organization.

> ## Make the most of yourself,
> ## for that is all there is of you.
> *Ralph Waldo Emerson, American philosopher and writer*

Participant ➤ Manager ➤ Leader

The development of a leader is an evolutionary process. Most leaders begin their careers as participants; paid employees or committee volunteers. Then they become department managers or committee chairpersons. After they've been on the job long enough for others to appreciate their values, their passion, and their ability to create, plan, and execute, they are promoted to leadership positions.

The evolution from participant to leader is an organic process, with each step building on what came before. You don't stop doing lower-level work when you become a manager, and you don't stop managing as you rise up the leadership ladder. In the hundreds of associate attitude surveys I've read, one of the top five qualities that associates most respect in a leader is his or her willingness to pitch in when the situation demands it. Pretenders look on subordinate jobs as being beneath their dignity. Genuine Leaders often step back into managerial or employee roles during vacations, unexpected terminations, or spikes in business. You shouldn't forget where you came from.

As an organization grows, the time a leader spends leading grows, too. Here is an example of how additional responsibilities may result in different amounts of time spent leading, managing, or working as an associate.

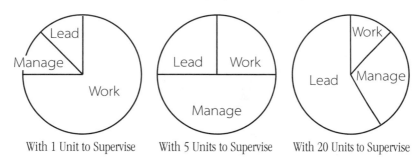

| With 1 Unit to Supervise | With 5 Units to Supervise | With 20 Units to Supervise |

New leaders need to remember the employee and manager roles they've played in the past and will continue to play in the future. The amount of time you spend leading, managing or working on a typical day will vary from organization to organization.

A leader shouldn't lose his or her personal touch. People need to see their leader involved in all levels of the company. Management expert W. Edwards Deming said that a leader should practice "management by walking around." In other words, a leader shouldn't sit in the office isolating himself or herself from the rank-and-file members of the company. Associates should be accustomed to seeing their leader visiting their work areas on a regular basis.

When the associates don't see their leader, they look for a surrogate to fill the void. In the history of the U.S. labor movement, unions moved into the gaps left by Pretenders who had distanced themselves from their people. A Genuine Leader walks the fine line between being available to his or her other associates while still being organizationally above them. He or she must be compassionate, approachable, knowledgeable, and trustworthy without being a buddy.

A leader should leave work at the end of the day more tired from verbally giving direction to others than physically tired from doing the work for them.

Genuine Leader

They want to follow you,
        not be your buddy or your equal.
You are their leader. They want someone
        in charge that they can trust...someone
they respect, someone they can be proud of.

General Colin Powell (Ret.), American statesman

Shifting Your Growth Curve

With time represented on the horizontal axis and profitability (or productivity) on the vertical axis, the Sigmoid Curve, shown below, is a graphic representation of how something in an organization is "born," grows, matures, and "dies".

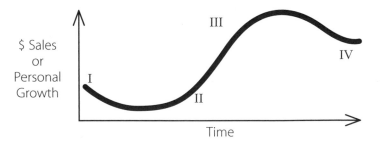

This curve can illustrate the life cycle of an industry, a company, a product, or even a leader. During Phase I, many mistakes, costs, and challenges can occur; hence, there is an initial downward (unproductive, unprofitable) dip in the S-curve. In Phase II, the entity on the curve begins to make strides and grows in a meaningful way. In Phase III, complacency and a sense of immortality may set in, causing profits, performance, and the growth curve to flatten. Phase IV shows the inevitable decline of the company, product, or career.

According to British executive and management educator Charles Handy, the secret of continued growth is to start a new Sigmoid Curve before the old one begins to decline. As Handy explains it, "The right place to start that second curve is at the point before the first curve begins to dip downwards," because at this point, the resources and energy needed to propel the new curve through its Phase I start-up challenges still exist. Handy depicts this optimal scenario with a second S-curve beginning before the inevitable decline of the first curve begins, as shown in the figure below at letter A.

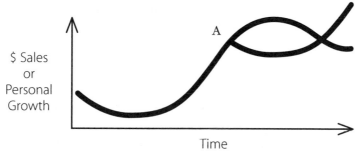

The Sigmoid Curve can be used as a timeline for a leader's career, starting with the moment of hiring, the orientation phase, the growth with promotions, the maturity period, and the inevitable retirement (physical or mental). When you continue to keep your options open by growing personally and intellectually, you'll be able to stay on top of your curve longer or shift to a new S-curve.

Let me give you three examples of how astute leaders created new S-curves for their 1. company, 2. product, or 3. personal career before their initial S-curves started to trend down.

1. Starbucks — Shifting a Company's S-curve

In our multi-tasking society, the popularity of fast food was quickly turning the cup of coffee at the local diner into an outdated custom. Enter Starbucks. The company single-handedly changed the world's coffee consumption by reinventing the coffee shop and transforming a common cup of java into a mood-altering experience. Starbucks's 19,000 possible permutations of coffees and flavorings, served by highly trained associates known as baristas, bear little resemblance to reheated joe from the corner greasy spoon.

2. Church & Dwight Co., Inc. — Arm & Hammer® Baking Soda — Shifting a Product's S-curve

As the 1970's approached, a product whose sole purpose depended on people baking at home faced obvious challenges. What does a company do when its main product caters to a bygone lifestyle? Shift the item's S-curve, of course.

The leadership at Church & Dwight repackaged Arm & Hammer as a cleaning and deodorizing product useful in the entire household, not just a baking ingredient. This shift resulted in one of the most successful marketing transformations ever made, and it moved Arm & Hammer from Phase IV on one curve to Phase I on a totally new curve. The product was given a broader definition and far greater sales potential.

3. Chris Castle, Production Manager – Shifting a Leader's S-curve

My half-brother Chris is a talented leader in the field of industrial manufacturing. Chris recognized that he was at the top of his career in the domestic market, so he began to study Japanese to place himself in a better position to take advantage of emerging opportunities in the international arena.

Through focused determination, countless hours of study, and lots of traveling, Chris was able to shift to an entirely new personal S-curve of international industrial manufacturing during the "sweet spot" of his career.

Genuine Leaders are not only aware of where their company is on its Sigmoid Curve, they are keen on the location they hold on their own S-curve. They continually reassess their plan to extend their curve or to shift to an entirely new one through continuous acts of self-development.

Quiet Time to Self-Develop

> ## The man who does not read good books has no advantage over the man who cannot.
> *Mark Twain, American author*

Self-development requires thought. As Socrates said, "An unexamined life is not worth living." We all need a place and time to think, to contemplate, to review our life and the direction it's taking. Thinking requires quiet time. Where do you find the most dependable quiet time to think? While driving? In the shower? Walking the dog? Mowing the lawn? Going for a run is my favorite opportunity for contemplation.

Some Pretenders program every minute of every day, often doing two or three things at once so they can always look busy and important. They equate down time or "think time" with being unproductive. Genuine Leaders, on the other hand, cherish their precious quiet time. Self-development and problem solving require uninterrupted moments of silence that allow thoughts to flow.

Henry Ford once said, "Thinking is hard work, and that's why people avoid it by surrounding themselves with noise." He should have seen the world we live in today! We watch an alarming amount of television. We let the radio drown out our thoughts while we drive. And now, with the proliferation of cell phones and MP3 players, it seems as though most people are constantly injecting noise directly into their brains. We live in a world that encourages and applauds multi-tasking. Conventional wisdom suggests that quiet time won't earn you any money, so you should talk on the cell phone while simultaneously walking on the treadmill and watching the latest news on television.

Genuine Leaders don't disturb their treasured quiet moments. They understand the importance of a timeout, and they often schedule it in their planners with the rest of their appointments. Some get up an hour early in the morning, while others set aside time right before bed. Whether it's in the form of a round of golf, a solitary walk, or keeping the office door closed for half an hour each afternoon, every Genuine Leader understands that "think time" is essential if he/she is going to be optimally effective.

Finding the Time

Finding the time for self-development isn't as difficult as Pretenders claim it is. In my first book, *It's About Time*, I suggest portioning the 168 hours in a week into four sections, like four slices of a pie. The first two, the hours devoted to the job and for sleep, are pretty much set in stone. The remaining hours are divided between living and self-development.

Of course, each of us slices our Pie of Life in our own way, but I recommend the following division:

WORK	55 hours
	(includes commuting time)
SLEEP	55 hours
LIVING	55 hours
SELF-DEVELOPMENT	3 hours
TOTAL	**168 hours in a week**

Allocating a set number of hours per week for self-development makes sense. After your formal education is over, the burden to continue learning falls directly onto you. Neither your parents nor your guidance counselor will be there to make sure you finish your homework. Once people get a job, their passion for continuing their formal education often seems to fall off a cliff. It's been said that a lot of people quit looking for work as soon as they find a job. Similarly, a lot of people stop learning as soon as they have a diploma. Genuine Leaders know that real learning begins after you leave the classroom.

Earl Nightingale, one of the pioneers of the 20th century's self-development movement, wrote that if you devote one hour per day to studying any single topic, within five years you will become a bona fide expert in that subject. How many hours a day do you waste? Can you spare one of those hours and use it to study a subject in depth? Of course you can.

> # Education is not the filling of a pail, but the lighting of a fire.
> *William Butler Yeats, Irish poet*

Leading by Example

Genuine Leaders rarely believe that they've reached the pinnacle of anything, and their humble demeanors demonstrate this attitude. They understand that they can always get better and learn something new. This quality has a powerful trickle-down effect within an organization. If Genuine Leaders demonstrate a penchant for learning and self-development, their associates will be more likely to do the same.

The leader of an organization is similar to a parent. Children emulate the actions of authority figures. If you love sports, your children will probably love them too. If you have bad habits, your children will adopt them. If you never read a book, look at a newspaper, or watch a documentary, your children will probably follow in your footsteps.

Corporate leaders who constantly demonstrate the necessity of learning are powerful role models for their associates. They offer incentives for continuing education. E-learning via the Internet has become the norm rather than the exception, and through this tool, information about business and personal development appears continually on the associate's computer in a variety of formats and difficulty levels. There's no excuse for any organization to avoid participating in education programs. If they forget education, they'll be left in their competitors' dust.

In an information society, education is no mere amenity; it's the prime tool for growing people and profits.

John Naisbitt and Patricia Aburdene, authors, "Megatrends"

Bob Cutler is the president of C3 – Creative Consumer Concepts, a company that designs restaurant marketing programs that target children. In his organization, he has combined his passion for volunteer work with his corporate influence to allow his associates to experience the benefits of charitable giving.

Over the years, Bob's volunteer work has included chairing committees, serving on boards of directors of charities, and going on overseas relief missions. He feels greatly enriched by going outside his world to make a difference in the lives of others, and he wants to offer his employees the same opportunity. Bob fully recognizes that Genuine Leaders develop both themselves and others. He created local and global community service programs for his associates, who are encouraged to take 40 paid hours a year doing volunteer work locally or abroad. Bob has found that when his associates volunteer to work for a worthy cause, they become more "others-focused." He says that this behavior eventually carries over into the workplace. By helping others, his associates accomplish great things, both with their co-workers and with the world at large.

Two of Bob's associates, Rachel and Joy, took the opportunity that he offered and traveled to Romania together to work in an orphanage. The young co-workers were stunned by what they saw on the very first day. They were assigned to different rooms that were each filled with babies. The orphanage's routine was to take the babies out of their cribs each morning, lay them on the floor, and return them to their cribs at night, with no physical human interaction during the entire day. Rachel and Joy sat on the floor to play with the babies, and they were extremely moved when the children crawled toward them and clung to them. Discovering the simple power of touch and a soothing voice was a life-altering experience for both of them.

When Bob's associates return from their volunteer efforts, they prepare and

6. Remember that your people will look at your commitment to self-development and to increasing your PAV.

What they see in you will influence their behavior and their propensity to want to grow. Be a positive influence.

> We cannot lead others
> to any other level of effectiveness
> than we are currently leading ourselves.
>
> *Steven Covey, self-help author*

RECOMMENDED READING

➤ Time Tactics of Very Successful People
by B. Eugene Griessman *(McGraw-Hill, 1994)*
➤ The Strangest Secret
by Earl Nightingale *(Reissue, B.N. Publishing, 2006)*
➤ Any books in the series: ___ *for Dummies* or *The Complete Idiot's Guide to* ___.
➤ It's About Time
by Harold C. Lloyd *(Pathways Education Program, 1996)*

Chapter Eight Appendix:

UPWARD EVALUATION PROCESS: SAMPLE FORM

Memo to: My Associates   From: _____

                                           (Leader's name)

                                           Date: _____

Re: Management's Annual Upward Evaluation

Please answer the following four questions. Your feedback will help the company grow. Expect to spend at least 15 minutes preparing and writing your answers. Please print your answers so they are legible. It's not necessary to sign your name. These surveys will be collected anonymously, and your valuable feedback will be handled respectfully and confidentially. Thank you for your candor.

Q1. In your opinion, what were our company's two most notable accomplishments during the last 12 months?
Accomplishment 1: _____
Accomplishment 2: _____

Q2. As a company, what should our two most important goals be for the next 12 months?
Goal 1: _____
Goal 2: _____

Q3. What two obstacles do you foresee that may prevent us from achieving the two goals above?
Obstacle 1: _____
Obstacle 2: _____

Q4. Please list at least two ways I should change to become a better leader for this company.
Change 1: _____
Change 2: _____

Name (Optional): _____
Date:_____

CHAPTER 9

GENUINE LEADERS ARE HEALTH CONSCIOUS

It's a struggle to lead when you feel sick in the head.
Even more of a challenge when you're sick in your bed.
And nearly impossible to lead
when you're lying down dead.
So take care of yourself.
Okay?
Enough said!

Genuine Leader

While on an airplane one night, I was reading an insurance industry article that gave newly-published life expectancy figures for someone living in the United States. The article announced that we could expect to live 77 years, up from 76 a few years before. At the time, I was 43 years old and 77 seemed a long way off. But then I grabbed a beverage napkin and began a mathematical exercise that changed my outlook on life and inspired me to write a book about time management. When I subtracted 43 from 77 and multiplied the difference (34) by 365, I discovered that my life expectancy at that moment was a mere 12,410 days. This number seemed incredibly puny to me, and I immediately resolved to adopt a healthier lifestyle. If I was only going to live to the age of 77, I wouldn't be able to see or do a lot of what I had planned for the rest of my life.

If you do this little mathematical exercise, you might appreciate each day a little bit more, and perhaps you'll begin to lead a healthier life, which benefits both yourself and those with whom you want to spend your time.

When you mention healthy living to some people, they immediately think of marathon runners or decathletes. For the purposes of this chapter, we'll refer to being health conscious as understanding the impact that eating, sleeping, and exercise have on maintaining a clear mind, unbridled enthusiasm, and the energy to lead others.

I truly enjoy leading a classroom of eager students, but when I'm unable to exercise in the morning, a three-hour class can sometimes be more of a chore than a thrill.

As a businessperson, there's nothing more exciting than a grand opening. However, the months of preparation, the weeks of execution, and the days of sleep deprivation can often drain the exhilaration out of that climatic moment when the ribbon is finally cut. Exercise and other healthy regimens will help keep you enthusiastic, even in the most stressful of situations.

Genuine Leaders understand that their body is the vehicle taking them from Project A to Problem B to Solution C. And if that vehicle hasn't been properly maintained, it can be very difficult to get to the right place at the right time. The most important relationship you can have in your lifetime is the one you have with your own health. And it's your ultimate responsibility. Your significant others are counting on your emotional and physical well-being.

Over the last 15 years, I've consciously adopted habits to improve my health and prolong my existence. The catalyst for this initiative was my family. I knew if I wanted to be around to see their lives unfold, I needed to lead a healthier life. To accomplish this goal, I've been adding at least one new healthy behavior each year. By continuously layering healthier habits into my lifestyle, I could, over time, increase my Personal Asset Value for my family, myself, and my business associates.

The first new behavior that I adopted was to begin flossing daily. I learned the importance of this vital habit from a new dental hygienist who gave my gums a grade of C minus. She told me that 90% of people over the age of 50 suffer from serious gum disease because they didn't floss every day. Overnight I became an avid flosser. Years later, I read *You: The Owner's Manual* by Dr. Mehmet Oz and Dr. Michael Roizen. Lo and behold, the authors said that daily flossing adds over six years to your life.

Once I'd established my flossing routine, I learned about the importance of drinking a sufficient amount of water each day. The amount of water that I had been drinking on a daily basis was about half the amount recommended. Good old-fashioned water is necessary for your physical and mental well-being. Because the brain is comprised mostly of water, you need proper hydration for it to perform at its best. Drinking the recommended six to eight glasses of water each day is more important than most people realize. Nerve cells transmit impulses via electricity. Water is the conductor that allows these transmissions to take place. When cells become dehydrated, their ability to function decreases dramatically.

Over the years, I've also made major adjustments in my exercise routine. The body needs exercise for many reasons. The brain relies on blood for nourishment. If there's more blood that is available to the brain, it can think, create, reason, and problem-solve more easily. Aerobic activity increases and enhances the body's ability to transport blood and thus carry oxygen to the brain. By becoming more aerobically fit, your body can supply more oxygen to the brain.

When it comes to exercise, I used to make excuses. If the weather wasn't just right, I'd put it off to the next day. So I created "weather-proof" and "excuse-proof" exercise alternatives: a bike ride on warm days, free weights on rainy days, a run on cool days, etc. Now, I have an option for every day. No excuses.

Many of the nation's most successful business leaders understand the need for exercise. Some, like Charles "Chuck" Ledsinger, CEO of Choice Hotels International, are dedicated runners. When Ledsinger can't run, he chooses to walk up the stairs instead of taking the elevator. Mark Freitas, president and CEO of Altiga Networks, is so devoted to good health that he insists that his employees adopt healthy habits as well. He'll take a 5-to-10 mile run instead of sitting down to a big business lunch. On the road, he stays in hotels that offer treadmills in their fitness rooms. He doesn't let a busy work schedule interfere with his workout schedules. As he says, "I learned a number of years ago that to be productive, I had to be physically active."

We are under-exercised as a nation.
We watch instead of play. We ride instead of walk.
Our existence deprives us of the minimum
physical activity essential for healthy living.

John F. Kennedy, American president

Another healthy upgrade I made was to improve my sleep habits. I used to consider myself awake and fully rested after four to five hours of sleep. I often hear people boast that they can "get by on only four hours of sleep." While this may be true for a very small percentage of the population, most of us require far more sleep. In fact, the National Sleep Foundation recommends that adults need from seven to nine hours of sleep per night. Furthermore, "getting by" is hardly a commendable goal. Instead of merely aiming to survive, we should aim to thrive.

Randy Fields, a co-founder of Mrs. Fields Cookies and the CEO of Park City

Group, told *Forbes* magazine that he uses meditation and yoga to de-stress so that he can get a good night's sleep. I keep a notebook and a pen on the nightstand next to my bed. If I wake up after four hours because of an idea or a dream, I can immediately write it down and go back to sleep. Those last few hours are crucial for the brain to get the rest it needs.

The best bridge between despair and hope is a good night's sleep.

E. Joseph Cossman, American salesman and entrepreneur

My Mentor – Jerry

Throughout my childhood, my two father figures were very poor mentors. My natural father was an alcoholic, and my stepfather was a workaholic. Luckily, I met Jerry, who became my "adopted" father and mentor. Jerry was an executive vice-president of a mid-sized corporation. After reading about each other's companies in the trade press, we became pen pals. By coincidence, I ended up living in Jerry's hometown, Virginia Beach, Virginia.

For 12 years, Jerry and I met monthly for breakfast to talk about business, investments, and life in general. Jerry's good advice guided me throughout those years. On numerous occasions, his wisdom and experience greatly influenced my personal and business decisions. He encouraged me to start a business locally so that I wouldn't have to travel so much. Jerry said that the time he'd spent away from his family early in his career had had a negative effect on many aspects of his life.

In the lobby of my first restaurant, I hung a plaque dedicating the business to Jerry. My only regret was that Jerry couldn't attend the grand opening of the business that he had urged me to start. A few months earlier, he had passed away due to serious health issues. But even in death, Jerry continued to mentor me by demonstrating that I should keep up a healthy lifestyle.

Jerry used to tease me about my exercise routine. He once said, "The day I see a jogger smiling is the day I'll start exercising." Jerry lacked an exercise routine and ignored proper eating and drinking practices throughout most of his life. Jerry's only shortcoming as a Genuine Leader was his poor health regimen.

Jerry's death opened my eyes to how important a Genuine Leader's health is to his/her ability to lead. Perhaps Jerry would have died when he did even if he had eaten properly and exercised daily. I'll never know. What I do know is that his incredible talent to lead others was cut short much too soon.

Optimistic Thinking

> Don't tell other people your problems.
> 80% of them don't care... and the other 20%
> are glad you have them.
>
> *Lou Holtz, American football coach*

If you're running a company in a competitive industry where you must deal with a board of directors, impatient stockholders, and many teams who need constant guidance, it's easy to fall into the pit of pessimism. Pretenders see the cup as half empty. They picture the light at the end of the tunnel as an express train heading in their direction.

Pretenders' negative thinking is reflected in the rest of the organization and wears away the health of the leader. Pessimism leads to stress, and both of these factors have been linked directly to a variety of ailments that could cause an early death.

> If you make every game a life and death
> proposition, you'll be dead a lot.
>
> *Dean Smith, college basketball coach*

There are dozens of ways to change your attitude from depressed to upbeat. Daniel G. Amen, M.D., wrote a book called *Change Your Brain, Change Your Life,* in which he suggests that we all re-read Ellen Porter's classic children's book *Pollyanna.* The title character is an 11-year-old orphan who is sent to live with her stern aunt. Although her life is grim, Pollyanna always finds a way to turn her lemons into lemonade. Even the worst situation has a sunny side. If you're depressed on a Monday morning, Pollyanna will remind you to be happy because it's a whole seven days until Monday comes around again.

Pollyanna explains that her late father taught her how "to find something about everything to be glad about – no matter what 'twas." Dr. Amen says that everyone should emulate her attitude and always look for the silver lining. "There are many different ways to look at a situation," he says. "If you're always looking for the bad in things, then you're going to be anxious and depressed, and your brain won't work as well. What you think and the spin you put on your life matters."

I've often heard pessimistic people say, "I can't help it. That's the way I think." Fortunately, they're wrong. According to Martin E. P. Seligman, Ph.D., professor of psychology at the University of Pennsylvania, optimism can be learned just like any other skill. He points out that every human being faces the same tragedies and setbacks. The optimist is resilient and bounces back. The pessimist falls into depression.

In his bestselling book, *Learned Optimism*, Seligman gives step-by-step advice about how to turn your attitude around. He says, "Because of his resilience, the optimist achieves more at work, at school and on the playing field…has better physical health and may even live longer." As the British comedy troupe Monty Python puts it, "Always look on the bright side of life!"

Seek to be defined by how you handle adversity.

Chris Castle, businessman (and my half brother)

SUMMARY SCORE:

How well are you taking care of yourself? Do you eat sensibly, get enough sleep and exercise regularly? Are you careful about your health habits? Are you making a conscientious effort to increase your own PAV by being a healthy individual?

Score yourself on a scale of 1-10

Recommendations to Raise Your *Health Conscious* Score:

1. **From now on, recognize that the phrase "you look tired" is not a compliment.**

For years, I interpreted this remark as being synonymous with working hard. But "you're such a hard worker" is vastly different from "you look tired." The distinction hit me on the day when someone guessed my age was 5 years more than it actually was. Of course, occasionally looking tired because of a stressful situation is unavoidable. But if you have constant bags under your eyes, your lifestyle is probably not healthy. Genuine Leaders recognize that the comment "you look tired" is a cue to alter their priorities so that they can get back into balance and be well rested.

2. Read the book *You: The Owner's Manual* by Dr. Mehmet Oz and Dr. Michael Roizen.

I hope the habits that I've shared with you have piqued your interest, but it's always better to consider more than one opinion and get professional advice. *You: The Owner's Manual* offers many compelling suggestions for you to consider.

3. Have a complete physical examination regularly.

Thinking that it's a waste of time to get a physical when nothing seems wrong might turn out to be a deadly mistake.

4. Create your own Once-A-Year Physical Health Improvement Plan.

For instance, you could start with the goal of flossing daily, then acclimate yourself to drinking six eight-ounce glasses of water per day, and so on. Year after year, you will be building a healthier lifestyle. It's a slow process, but the rewards are huge.

How old would you be if you didn't know how old you were?

Leroy "Satchel" Paige, American baseball player

RECOMMENDED READING:

➡ YOU: The Owner's Manual: An Insider's Guide to the Body that Will Make You Healthier and Younger

by Michael F. Roizen, M.D. and Mehmet Oz, M.D. *(Collins Publishing, 2005)*

➡ YOU on a DIET: The Owner's Manual for Waist Management

by Michael F. Roizen, M.D. and Mehmet Oz, M.D. *(Free Press, 2006)*

➡ Power Sleep: The Revolutionary Program That Prepares Your Mind for Peak Performance

by James B. Maas *(Collins, 1999)*

➡ Learned Optimism: How to Change Your Mind and Your Life

by Martin E.P. Seligman, Ph.D. *(Free Press; Reissue edition, 1998)*

CHAPTER 10

Genuine Leaders Maintain a Family Focus

The strength of a nation derives
from the integrity of the home.

Confucius, ancient Chinese philosopher

that "men are more likely than women to quit their jobs if time with their kids is jeopardized." Microsoft's founder, Bill Gates, says, "Having kids has been a fantastic thing for me. Its meant that I'm a little more balanced. In my twenties I worked massively. I hardly took vacations at all. Now, with the help of my wife, I'm always making sure I've got a good balance of how I spend my time."

> It's all about quality of life and finding a happy balance between work and friends and family.
>
> *Sir Philip Green, British retailer*

Steve Reinemund, who retired in 2007 as Chairman of the Board of PepsiCo, had a 23-year history with the company. Reinemund has four children, and his first consideration in any career decision is what's best for his family. This has required a number of tradeoffs during his long career with PepsiCo. When he was the head of Pizza Hut, he turned down the opportunity to take over the much larger Kentucky Fried Chicken division because the move wasn't in his family's best interest.

When he took over as PepsiCo CEO, he returned his family to Dallas and he commuted to the company's Purchase, New York headquarters. Reinemund explained it this way. "My success model is like a chair with four legs. In the center is God. Family, friends, community and work are the four legs."

> In the annals of world history, there is no record of anyone on their deathbed ever saying, "I wish I'd spent more time at the office."
>
> *Paul Tsongas, U.S. Senator*

So you won't be terribly disappointed at the end of your life, let me be the bearer of some tough news. The truth is, the size of your funeral will be in direct relation to the weather that day. That's right. Forget all the pondering you've done about the size of your funeral and those people who owe it to you to attend. It doesn't mean anything.

I'm writing this the day after attending a wake for a friend's husband. It was a bitter cold evening and I'm convinced that some people, probably very close to the deceased and his family, chose not to attend because of the weather.

These people simply weighed their options and chose to do something they would find more comfortable than going out into the freezing night.

The genuinely important people in your life give your life true meaning. There are only a select few who cherish your existence. In no way should these wonderful people be given a disproportionately small share of your time. Protect their slice of your life. The others don't matter nearly as much.

Life: Enter it seeking balance, leave feeling fulfilled.

Carol L. Christison, Executive Director, IDDBA

Here's how I look at it. Someone will always have more money than you. Someone will always have more things than you. Someone may even have a better job than you. But nobody can ever take credit for YOUR family or YOUR friends.

The quality of both your family and your friendships will reflect the time and effort that you put into them. "Quality time" is not enough. You need quantities of time as well.

It's not enough to make time for your children. There are certain stages in their lives when you have to give them the time when they want it. You can't run your family like a company. It doesn't work.

Andrew Grove, retired chairman, Intel Corporation

SUMMARY SCORE:

How well do you integrate your personal life with your business activities? How many true friends do you have; that is, people who applaud your achievements and enjoy your friendship without ulterior motives?

Score yourself on a scale of 1-10

Recommendations to Grow Your *Family Focus* Score:

1. Use "Stay Focused" index cards as reminders.

On several 3 x 5-inch index cards, write or type the six or seven most important and meaningful things in your life, e.g., work, religion, education, family, exercise, etc. Tape these cards near any phone you use, on your bathroom mirror, and on your dashboard; also, stash a card in your wallet. Whenever anyone asks you to do something that requires an investment of your time, think about your priorities. If the request can be linked to one of your "stay focused" priorities, feel free to accept the invitation. If it doesn't, politely decline the request.

We're all limited by the number of hours in our day and the number of days in our lives. That's why it's up us to make sure that we allocate the proper amount of time to the priorities in our lives. This principle is especially important for family time because families are frequently taken for granted and can be short-changed all too often.

2. Utilize the Parent's Report Card.

Every couple of years, ask your children to complete this Parent's Report Card on you and your spouse. Their feedback should offer valuable points of discussion to grow your relationship with them.

PARENT'S REPORT CARD

My Mother/Father...	Excellent	Good	Fair	Poor	Fail
1. Is Honest and Always Tells the Truth	A	B	C	D	F
2. Has Worked Hard to Make Us a Close Family	A	B	C	D	F
3. Listens Carefully to My Problems	A	B	C	D	F
4. Keeps Promises	A	B	C	D	F
5. Promotes Healthy Living	A	B	C	D	F
6. Gives Understandable, Helpful Advice	A	B	C	D	F
7. Takes the Time to Teach Me Things	A	B	C	D	F
8. Does Not Embarrass Me in Front of My Friends	A	B	C	D	F
9. Provides an Optimistic/Upbeat Outlook on Things	A	B	C	D	F
10. Provides for All Our Needs	A	B	C	D	F
11. Is Fair When Disciplining Me and Does Not Lose Control	A	B	C	D	F

12. Has Taught Me How to Make Good Decisions	A	B	C	D	F
13. Encourages Me to Be a Good Citizen and Good to the Environment	A	B	C	D	F
14. Is a Very Positive Influence on Me	A	B	C	D	F
15. Is Easy to Respect and Trust	A	B	C	D	F

Scoring: A=4, B=3, C=2, D=1, F=0

Your Score:_____ (Is your score sufficient? Only you can say.)

3. Use and enjoy your vacation time and encourage others to do the same.

Quality rest and relaxation will make you more focused when you return to the workplace.

4. Analyze the quality of your friendship.

Periodically ask yourself, "Would I like having me as a friend?" If your answer makes you feel uneasy, then make the necessary adjustments in your life and/or personality.

I wouldn't want to belong to any club that would have me as a member.

Groucho Marx, American actor and comedian

RECOMMENDED READING

➥ **Dare to Be True: Living in the Freedom of Complete Honesty**
by Mark D. D. Roberts *(Waterbrook Press, 2003)*
➥ **The One Minute Manager Balances Work and Life**
by Ken Blanchard and Marjorie Blanchard *(Harper Paperbacks, 1999)*
➥ **Life Matters: Creating a Dynamic Balance of Work, Family, Time & Money**
by A. Roger Merrill and Rebecca Merrill *(McGraw-Hill, 2003)*
➥ **The Friendship Factor: How to Get Closer to the People You Care for**
by Alan Loy McGinnis *(Augsburg Fortress Publishers, 2004)*

CHAPTER 11

GENUINE LEADERS BRING FUN TO THE WORKPLACE

Laughter is shortest distance between two people.

Victor Borge, Danish humorist and musician

Many jobs become boring over time. And "over time" can often mean about two weeks. While people may not always be fond of change, they abhor monotonous repetition. One of the best methods to keep associates stimulated is to plan and execute events that give them Something To Look Forward To (STLFT).

I have always believed that you can't truly motivate people to do something they don't enjoy doing. Instead, try to create a work environment that engages the associates' interest so they motivate themselves.

If you want a quick reality check, ask your associates how many of them always look forward to the weekend. Once you face the fact that most of them prefer weekends to coming to work, you might ponder what they look for outside of the workplace that they can't get during the work week. The answer is FUN. Unfortunately, most of us don't have fun at work.

I know a small, successful company that has "fun" as a core company value. The company's mission is to help restaurants enhance their brands with marketing programs that target youngsters. Its internal goal is to create fun for its 40 associates.

Some of the fun they have happens spontaneously. For instance, on a hot day when management decided that everyone needed a break, they called an ice cream truck. When the truck arrived, the associates heard the music and ran out to the parking lot for free ice cream. The snack made them feel like kids again. Associates often toss water balloons back and forth or eat freshly cooked hamburgers from the company grill. Who wouldn't want to work for a company like that? Not surprisingly, their annual employee turnover rate is less than one-third of the national average for its industry.

Experience has taught me that associates tend to look forward to paydays, days off, and their vacation. Unfortunately, the positive impact of these three STLFTs for your company is minimal because virtually every job offers them. A Genuine Leader provides unique events, both planned and spontaneous, on a daily, weekly, and monthly basis. These activities give the employees STLFTs that make them want to come to work.

STLFT events are most effective when they're spread throughout the year at intervals of no longer than 30 days. The typical associate has, at most, a 30-day "span of interest." Anticipation and enthusiasm fall off dramatically for events more than a month away. Whenever we held an STLFT event, I would hear associates enthusiastically talking about it a week or two in advance, and they'd continue to talk about it for two weeks after the event. Consequently, we would get a 30-day spike in employee enthusiasm for every major activity we ran.

One of my favorite STLFT promotions was our annual Pet Event. We encouraged our associates to dress up as their favorite animals to market the truckloads of pet food and pet paraphernalia that we planned to sell. Our customers could enter their pets in one of 10 categories for prizes. One year, we had a pair of geese that waddled through the store. They were dressed in wedding outfits: top hat and tails for the gander, and a white wedding dress and train for the goose. Both associates and customers talked for weeks about these geese as well as the many other costumes they had seen. We engaged our customers, sold piles of merchandise and achieved a month's worth of above-average associate enthusiasm.

Associates who are having fun have a better mental attitude, which produces endorphins. These chemicals increase oxygen and blood flow to the brain. Thus, happy employees can think more creatively, which benefits the entire organization.

Pretender

When you're in jail, a good friend will be trying to bail you out. But a BEST friend will be in the cell next to you saying, "Damn, that was fun!"

Not every associate will be jazzed by every event, but enough of them will have enough fun to make the event worthwhile. The alternative to an STLFT program is a boring, mundane workplace where your associates watch the clock rather than the calendar in anticipation of an upcoming event. Genuine Leaders know that most associates love surprises when they are fun, funny, thoughtful, or rewarding. A carefully-crafted and professionally-executed STLFT program can do wonders for a company's morale.

> Celebrate your successes.
> Find some humor in your failures.
> Loosen up and everybody around you
> will loosen up.
> Have fun. Show enthusiasm always.
>
> *Sam Walton, founder, Wal-Mart*

The cost of having fun at work is a lot like the cost of associate training. In the short term, it is an expense, but in the long term, it's a sound investment that pays off. Contrary to what Pretenders believe, having Fun and acting Professional do not conflict. Neither does having Fun and being Productive. Having fun in the workplace can be justified with the following sequence that draws a cause-and-effect connection between Fun (#1) and Results (#7).

1st → Fun makes a situation more enjoyable.

2nd → An enjoyable work environment invites associate participation.

3rd → When people participate they generally become more interested.

4th → Greater interest expands awareness.

5th → More awareness increases knowledge.

6th → Knowledge facilitates action.

7th → Action versus inaction produces more results.

Following this logic, it's evident that Fun yields seven distinctive organizational benefits and it produces Results.

SUMMARY SCORE:

Give yourself one point for each day out of 10 that you bring fun into your organization. Do you allow every day to be a repeat of the day before? Or are you a Genuine Leader who infuses levity, frivolity, humor, and fun into every day? If your score is high, you probably hear occasional laughter and see lots of smiles at work. You probably also have a high volunteer percentage for projects and a lower than average associate turnover rate.

Score yourself on a scale of 1-10

Recommendations to Raise Your *Bring Fun to the Workplace* Score:

1. Remember, "He who laughs, lasts."

Get in the habit of committing random acts of the unexpected in your organization every day.

2. Establish an STLFT Committee.

This group will create a calendar of scheduled fun and engaging events.

3. Make sure that your annual associate attitude survey contains a few questions that assess the degree of fun your associates have on the job.

Include questions such as "I look forward to coming to work each day," or "You never know what to expect; there is always something fun going on."

RECOMMENDED READING

➡ Fun Is Good: How To Create Joy & Passion in Your Workplace & Career by Mike Veeck and Pete Williams *(Rodale Books, 2005)*

➡ Managing to Have Fun: How Fun at Work Can Motivate Your Employees, Inspire Your Coworkers, and Boost Your Bottom Line by Matt Weinstein *(Fireside, 1997)*

CHAPTER 12

GENUINE LEADERS RECOGNIZE THE MOMENT OF TRUTH

All my life I've wanted to be somebody;
I realize now that I
should have been more specific.

Lily Tomlin, American comedian and actor

So, What's Your LQ?

You are undoubtedly familiar with an IQ, which is the measure of a person's intelligence. The test measures the ratio of your mental age versus your chronological age and multiplies it by 100. Human IQs fall along a bell curve from 0 and 200, with 80 percent of the population between 80 and 120.

You've also probably heard of EQ, which stands for Emotional Quotient. Popularized in the 1990s by Daniel Goleman, your EQ refers to your interpersonal skills; that is, your ability or capacity to perceive, assess, and manage your own emotions as well as those of others. Goleman breaks down emotional skills into the categories of self-awareness, self-management, social awareness, and relationship management.

And now, after many pages of reading, thinking and self-assessing, you're ready to successfully calculate your Leadership Quotient – your LQ.

Your LQ is the sum total of all ten leadership criteria outlined in the first ten chapters, plus the bonus points you received in Chapter 11 for bringing fun into the workplace.

Compare this number with the benchmark score that you gave yourself at the beginning of this book, where I asked you to estimate your ability to lead others on a scale of 1 – 100. If you were brutally honest with yourself, and if this LQ assessment process accurately measures your ability to lead, the numbers should be close. Take a look:

Your Initial Estimate = _____   *vs.* Your Calculated LQ = _____

If you're truly serious about effectively leading others, your LQ should be as important to you as your IQ, your EQ, your body temperature, and your blood pressure. Like the rest of these critical numbers, you should periodically measure and try to improve your LQ.

Now, let's look at your calculated LQ score. At this point, it's really unimportant whether you scored a 68 or an 86. What is much more important is what your LQ will be next year. To me, an 86 that was an 86 last year isn't nearly as exciting as a 68 that was a 54 last year.

This book's primary objective was to help you quantify your ability to lead. Although you may have had performance reviews in the past, its unlikely you've ever measured your ability to lead. Now, we've done that. We've calculated your Leadership Quotient. But you can't stop here. It's now time to *raise* your LQ.

Set S.M.A.R.T. Goals to Raise Your LQ

I've always believed in picking the "low hanging fruit" first. When you accomplish something sooner rather than later, you build confidence and momentum. In this case, the "low hanging fruit" represents your lowest LQ values, which I suggest you identify and attack. Let's say *Communication* and *Health Consciousness* are your lowest scores. Your next step should be to craft some S.M.A.R.T. goals that, when executed, will improve your score for those criteria by at least two points.

For example, to raise your *Communication* score, write a S.M.A.R.T. goal to enroll in a public speaking class this year. Or write one to introduce a more structured open door policy for your organization within the next 30 days. For your *Health Consciousness* initiative, write a S.M.A.R.T. goal to join a health club within the next two weeks and commit to a 30-minute-per-day, three-day-a-week workout routine. Your second goal might be to discontinue eating or snacking after 7:30 p.m. When you achieve these goals within the next 12 months, you will have a positive impact on the two criteria where your scores were lowest.

Working on two criteria per year while using S.M.A.R.T. goals should generate four or five additional LQ points for you annually. This will contribute to a significant and permanent improvement in your overall ability to lead others over time.

But are you ready to commit to change?
You can make it happen
or just happen to make it.
Your call.

Genuine Leader

Discretionary Effort

If the growth of your own Personal Asset Value isn't enough incentive to raise your LQ score, consider the concept of Discretionary Effort; that is, the amount of additional work produced by an individual after he/she has completed their required tasks.

Discretionary Effort can take the form of the extra sale a clerk made when he came back from a break a few minutes early to accommodate an anxious customer. It is shown by the staffer who cleaned up the break room when others had gone home. And Discretionary Effort is personified by a member of a softball team who spends an extra 30 minutes each practice to improve her hitting.

Your associates have complete control over when and where they'll produce Discretionary Effort. The amount they will give is dramatically affected by the quality of leadership they receive. Genuine Leaders know the importance of creating a supportive, challenging, and stimulating work environment to coax Discretionary Effort out of their associates. They know that Discretionary Effort can't be mandated – by definition, it's totally voluntary. If you consciously raise your LQ throughout your career, you'll develop into a Genuine Leader who taps into your associates' willingness to expend their Discretionary Effort.

Since your most valuable asset is the people who look up to you, don't be selfish with this LQ assessment process. Help your associates measure and develop their own LQs.

The haves and the have-nots
can often be traced back to
the dids and the did-nots.

Author Unknown

Are You the Leader You Need to Be?

A 93-year-old man was walking down a dirt road. A frog on the edge of the road said, "Pick me up, take me to town and I'll grant you three wishes." The old man bent down and picked up the frog and stuffed him directly into his pocket. The frog said, "Hey, buddy, what about your three wishes?" The old man replied, "At 93, a talking frog is enough for me."

Let's say you're 48 years old and your LQ is 84. Do you really need to change? After all, 84 is a good score. And at 48, you might feel like you're at or near the top of your game, and you might think that if you play your cards right, you could effectively ride out the rest of your career.

My guess is, whatever age you are, you're not ready to rest on your laurels. If you haven't made an aggressive effort to grow your LQ until now, you simply didn't know exactly where to begin. Now, after working through the chapters in this book and determining your LQ, you know where to begin and what needs to be done. So, get going and good luck!

It's never too late to be who you might have been.

George Eliot, British novelist

RECOMMENDED READING

➡ The Leadership Quotient: 12 Dimensions for Measuring and Improving Leadership
by Dave Arnott and Bill Service *(iUniverse, Inc., 2006)*
➡ Harvard Business Review on Breakthrough Leadership
by Daniel Goleman, William Peace, William Pagonis, Tom Peters, Gareth Jones, and Harris Collingwood
(Harvard Business School Press, 2002)

So, get going and good luck!